Editor-in-Chief

NEW DIRECTIONS FOR YOUTH DEVELOPMENT

Theory
Practice
Research

summer | 2004

Negotiation

Interpersonal Approaches to Intergroup Conflict

Daniel L. Shapiro
Brooke E. Clayton

issue
editors

Foreword by **Roger Fisher**

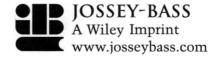

JOSSEY-BASS
A Wiley Imprint
www.josseybass.com

NEGOTIATION: INTERPERSONAL APPROACHES TO INTERGROUP CONFLICT
Daniel L. Shapiro, Brooke E. Clayton (eds.)
New Directions for Youth Development, No. 102, Summer 2004
Gil G. Noam, Editor-in-Chief

Microfilm copies of issues and articles are available in 16mm and 35mm, as well as microfiche in 105mm, through University Microfilms Inc., 300 North Zeeb Road, Ann Arbor, Michigan 48106-1346.

NEW DIRECTIONS FOR YOUTH DEVELOPMENT (ISSN 1533-8916, electronic ISSN 1537-5781) is part of The Jossey-Bass Psychology Series and is published quarterly by Wiley Subscription Services, Inc., A Wiley company, at Jossey-Bass, 989 Market Street, San Francisco, California 94103-1741. POSTMASTER: Send address changes to New Directions for Youth Development, Jossey-Bass, 989 Market Street, San Francisco, California 94103-1741.

SUBSCRIPTIONS cost $80.00 for individuals and $160.00 for institutions, agencies, and libraries. Prices subject to change. Refer to the order form at the back of this issue.

EDITORIAL CORRESPONDENCE should be sent to the Editor-in-Chief, Dr. Gil G. Noam, Harvard Graduate School of Education, Larsen Hall 601, Appian Way, Cambridge, MA 02138 or McLean Hospital, 115 Mill Street, Belmont, MA 02478.

Cover photograph by Digital Vision.

www.josseybass.com

Contents

Foreword

FOR THE PAST forty years, I have worked to improve the way that people deal with their differences. I was inspired by the awful consequences of World War II. After spending several years in the U.S. Army Air Force during the war, I returned home to discover that my roommate, two of my close friends, and many classmates had been killed in that war. I remember thinking to myself, "There has to be a better way for people to deal with their differences."

At the Harvard Negotiation Project, we developed interest-based negotiation, a collaborative approach to negotiation. In essence, we believe that peace is more than a piece of paper; it is a process for dealing nonviolently with differences. Rather than arguing over positions, people in conflict can come to understand one another's interests and work collaboratively to deal with them. Effective negotiation can generate mutually satisfying agreements without the need for any party to "give in" to the demands of the other.

The interest-based approach has been captured in a widely circulated book I coauthored: *Getting to YES: Negotiating Agreement Without Giving In.* The approach has been put to use in international relations, labor-management disputes, and even marital conflict.

Young people around the globe urgently need to learn the skills of dealing with differences. With the end of the Cold War, our world has changed. Terrorism and civil conflict destabilize each of the major continents. The power of young people to change our world was never more possible, or more important. They need to learn nonviolent ways to deal with their differences.

For the past several years, I have been coauthoring a book with Daniel Shapiro that focuses on how to deal with emotions in negotiation. I have embraced that project out of a belief in the power

NEW DIRECTIONS FOR YOUTH DEVELOPMENT, NO. 102, SUMMER 2004 © WILEY PERIODICALS, INC.

of the human dimension of negotiation. More than ever before, we need effective methods of coping with conflict that help people build constructive relationships and manage their emotions effectively.

It is with that backdrop that my colleagues Daniel Shapiro and Brooke Clayton have put together this urgently needed issue of *New Directions for Youth Development*. The chapters in this issue illustrate some of the innovative approaches being used around the world to help people deal with differences. What I find most impressive is the emphasis in each chapter on the importance of relationships. Whether in Burundi or Northern Ireland, there is great power in the ability to turn adversaries into colleagues working together side by side.

I strongly recommend this issue for anyone who has a desire to change the world for the better.

Roger Fisher

ROGER FISHER *is Professor Emeritus, Harvard Law School, and director of the Harvard Negotiation Project.*

Editors' Notes

TODAY'S YOUTH are growing up in a complicated world of politics, social tensions, and violent conflict. The cold war world, in which states focused on defending their borders from external intrusion, has been transformed. In its place is a dynamic, international fusion in which old threats are anachronistic and new threats are born. Since the end of the cold war, there has been a significant number of intrastate conflicts, with over forty currently taking place around the world. We now grapple with terrorism and localized violence; over 20 million men, women, and children are wartime refugees and internally displaced people.

Nowhere are such problems more apparent than between and among ethnicities, nationalities, religions, and other identity-based groups. From Northern Ireland to South Africa, youth confront the constant challenges of complex intergroup conflict. Members of one group treat members of the other group as adversaries simply because of their perceived identity as Hutu or Tutsi, Jew or Muslim. The group members tend to perceive the other side as an obstacle to the satisfaction of their own goals, values, safety, or resource needs.

When youth do not have the necessary skills to manage complex conflict effectively, serious consequences can result. In the short term, youth may fail to get their basic needs for food, water, shelter, or physical safety met, and the conflict can escalate to violence. Long-term consequences are equally pernicious. Youth grow up to be the decision makers of society, and if they lack adequate skills to deal with complex conflict, their limited ability to negotiate effectively may perpetuate violent conflict. A new generation of youth

NEW DIRECTIONS FOR YOUTH DEVELOPMENT, NO. 102, SUMMER 2004 © WILEY PERIODICALS, INC.

become victims of this violence, and sometimes they are its perpetrators. In either case, they tend to lack a feeling of human security—a sense of safety and empowerment that they can change their life circumstances for the better.

In this issue, we focus on three hypotheses to improve human security for youth (see Table A for a summary):

1. *Relationships are important.* A common assumption is that conflict management means solving a substantive problem. What are the terms of our agreement? However, conflicts take place within the frame of a relationship. Without addressing the relational aspects of conflict management, intergroup conflicts tend to recur. Faced with increasingly complex intergroup conflict, youth need effective skills to build constructive relationships.

2. *Relationships can improve, even during conflict.* If youth perceive that their relationship with the "other" is adversarial, it is likely that they will compete rather than cooperate, alienate rather than include, and assume rather than appreciate. By learning to build affiliation in the process of addressing conflict, youth gain the capacity to collaborate with many different kinds of people.

3. *Providing opportunities for intergroup interaction can help.* Building relationships requires time and teaching. Youth need appropriate settings where they can learn and practice the skills that will allow them to build affinity in the face of complex conflict.

Table A. Summary of diagnoses and strategies to deal with intergroup violence

Diagnosis	Strategy
Shortsighted goal: Focus on substantive solutions.	Expanded goal: Focus on substance and relationships.
Adversarial assumption: Relationships are seen as fixed and competitive.	Assumption of mutuality: Build affiliation while dealing cooperatively with differences.
Few opportunities: Lack of theory and interventions on relationship building for youth.	Provide opportunities: Give youth avenues to learn and practice relationship-building skills.

This issue of *New Directions for Youth Development* showcases a variety of innovative, effective conflict management interventions that implement the three hypotheses we have outlined.

In preparing for this issue, we circulated an international call for chapters. We wanted to attract a diverse group of scholars and practitioners engaged in conflict resolution work in varied regions of the world. Our intent was to convey a sense of the diversity and depth of the many approaches that are being implemented effectively worldwide. As a result, the chapter authors represent a broad spectrum of backgrounds and areas of interest. In tone and content, their chapters reflect the variation and uniqueness of their experiences and the richness of their individual perspectives.

Chapter One begins with an overview of two theoretical frameworks that have guided many conflict interventions. In applying those approaches to a group in Johannesburg, South Africa, Tricia Jones discovered that their effectiveness was conditional. She explores the application of an alternative model to help prepare youth for high-contact conflict interventions.

In Chapter Two, Marieke van Woerkom introduces one such conflict intervention. Seeds of Peace is a visionary international peace program targeting youth from some of the world's most intense, seemingly intractable conflicts. She focuses on the organization's first program, which brought together a group of Palestinian and Israeli youth for a transformative summer experience in Maine.

The Workable Peace program, described in Chapter Three, contrasts with interventions that bring students away from home. Stacie Nicole Smith and David Fairman emphasize the importance of integrating conflict management skills into school curricula. They describe the benefits and limitations of stand-alone programs, such as peer mediation programs or an elective on negotiation, and argue for the efficacy of integrated programs.

Recognizing the escalating ethnopolitical tensions immediately following the breakup of the Soviet Union, Daniel Shapiro developed a conflict management program intervention that now has reached close to 1 million youth throughout eastern and central

Europe. In Chapter Four, he describes its methodology, approach, and relevance in fostering an open society.

In Chapter Five, Jean-Paul Bigirindavyi develops a conflict management program in Burundi, one of the world's most inflamed sites of youth violence. The program seeks to engage youth through dialogue and civic participation.

Concluding this issue, Alan Smith and Ciarán Ó Maoláin offer a broad perspective on intergroup relations. They focus on the roots of intolerance and on approaches that have been used in educational systems and other areas of youth work to confront and challenge intolerance among young people.

Conflict management programs like the ones explored in this issue hold the potential to replace violence with peaceful means of dealing with differences. It is a daunting task, to be sure, but in the wise words of Krishnamurit, "A pebble can change the course of a river."

Daniel L. Shapiro
Brooke E. Clayton
Editors

DANIEL L. SHAPIRO *is an instructor in psychology in the Department of Psychiatry at Harvard Medical School/McLean Hospital and an associate at the Harvard Negotiation Project at Harvard Law School.*

BROOKE E. CLAYTON *is a student at Harvard Law School focusing on international development.*

Executive Summary

Chapter One: Enhancing collaborative tendencies: Extending the single identity model for youth conflict education

Tricia S. Jones

One of the most challenging aspects of conflict management is the reduction of prejudice that fuels destructive intergroup conflict. Parents, educators, and policymakers are searching for techniques that enhance the tendencies for collaboration, especially among youth engaged in intergroup conflicts related to cultural identification. In this chapter, reflections on a multicultural project in South Africa in the immediate postapartheid era suggest advantages of single identity work as an approach to prepare youth for collaboration.

Chapter Two: Seeds of Peace: Toward a common narrative

Marieke van Woerkom

Seeds of Peace has been called a detox program for youth from regions of conflict and war—youth who, at a very young age, have learned to distrust, fear, and even hate those on the other side of the political border. Through media, formal and informal education, family history, and tradition, many youth in countries of conflict have been raised to perceive their "enemy" as inhuman, making communication and constructive relationships impossible.

NEW DIRECTIONS FOR YOUTH DEVELOPMENT, NO. 102, SUMMER 2004 © WILEY PERIODICALS, INC.

Socialized in this way and carrying the baggage of war, these high-school-aged young people arrive at the Seeds of Peace International Camp in Maine, the starting point of a transformative journey that teaches an understanding of conflict, empathy for others, and a raised awareness of the conflict that, until then, has held them captive.

This chapter places the Seeds of Peace summer camp program in a wider educational context, providing an understanding of its programs and of the youth participating in them. The chapter begins with an overview of the program's history and then explores the context in which the youth participants have learned their misunderstandings. This analysis acts as a framework to introduce the Seeds of Peace program. The chapter discusses the dialogue component of the program, providing insight into the way in which Seeds of Peace challenges, encourages, and supports its participants to move toward a common narrative.

Chapter Three: Normalizing effective conflict management through academic curriculum integration: The example of Workable Peace

Stacie Nicole Smith, David Fairman

To become successful adults and effective global citizens, young people need to understand and respond effectively to personal, social, and political conflicts in their lives and in the world around them. Schools—as institutions charged with developing young people's knowledge, attitudes, behaviors, and skills for adulthood—are uniquely situated to address these needs. Issues of conflict and conflict management arise across the school curriculum and are particularly central in history and social studies courses. What knowledge, assumptions, and behaviors are students learning about conflict from their social studies classes? What else might we want them to learn?

This chapter argues that the teaching of skills for conflict management can and should be integrated into the standard high school curriculum. It offers an overview of the rationale for integration, discusses potential benefits and options, and examines traditional objections. It then describes specifically what skills such programs should be teaching, how they can be taught, and what difference they make, drawing on the theory and practice of dispute resolution and particularly on the authors' experiences with the Workable Peace project of the Consensus Building Institute. Finally, it explores barriers to integrating conflict resolution into the school curriculum and potential strategies for overcoming them.

Chapter Four: After the fall: A conflict management program to foster open society

Daniel L. Shapiro

This chapter describes the development of a conflict management program that has reached nearly 1 million youth in twenty-one former communist-bloc countries. With the fall of communism in eastern and central Europe, ethnopolitical tensions surfaced across the region. Beyond the urgent task of crisis management, an incredible amount of work was needed to support the transition from a closed to an open society. In this conflict management program, teachers and students learned skills and values necessary to deal effectively with one another within their new political, social, and economic infrastructure. This chapter provides an overview of the framework of the core curriculum and its relevance in postcommunist society.

Chapter Five: Youth Intervention for Peace Project: Burundi case study

Jean-Paul Bigirindavyi

The United Nations has identified Burundi as one of five countries where youth are most involved in the conduct of civil strife. Burundi faces the immediate and severe problem of constructing a society where young people have outlets for meaningful participation. In order to support recent peace agreements, communities and individuals need to be equipped with skills for the nonviolent resolution of differences. This chapter discusses the history of the perpetuation of violence in Burundi and the role of youth in it and analyzes how and why youth participate in ethnic conflict. Then it introduces the Youth Intervention for Peace Project, which aims to help youth break from patterns of violence through dialogue and community participation.

Chapter Six: Challenging intolerance

Alan Smith, Ciarán Ó Maoláin

The social identity of the individual is a complex layering, implicating many forms of group identification and differentiation. Conflict between groups is inevitable, and it is not always destructive; the challenging of one cultural form by another, and their creative interaction, can be a productive and positive dynamic of social life.

This chapter addresses the social control of conflict, and in particular, the macro- and microlevel strategies that address intolerance. It discusses the origin and nature of forms of intolerance within and between social groups and then examines approaches and techniques that have been used in educational systems, and in other areas of youth work, to confront and challenge intolerance among young people and to promote respect for diversity. Northern Ireland is the primary point of reference, but the chapter refers to many issues with a much wider relevance.

A conflict intervention in postapartheid South Africa suggests new insights into encouraging an honest and engaging participation in the dialogue process.

1

Enhancing collaborative tendencies: Extending the single identity model for youth conflict education

Tricia S. Jones

> Since wars begin in the minds of men, it is in the minds of men that the defenses of peace must be constructed.
> —Preamble of the Constitution of the United Nations, Educational, Scientific and Cultural Organization

PERHAPS MORE THAN EVER before, we need innovative and successful approaches to developing the defenses of peace in the minds of all humanity. We have witnessed the consequences of not attending to these needs in the many and varied international, interethnic, and intergroup conflicts around the globe. And while there are a variety of approaches to peace education, such as those that Ian Harris and Mary Lee Morrison have chronicled recently, we still know too little about how to encourage a peaceful orientation.[1]

My own reflections on these issues, prompted by two decades of work in conflict education, were stimulated during a three-year project in the Gauteng region of South Africa in the immediate

NEW DIRECTIONS FOR YOUTH DEVELOPMENT, NO. 102, SUMMER 2004 © WILEY PERIODICALS, INC.

postapartheid era.[2] In this chapter, I share some reflections on our successes and our missed opportunities and integrate those thoughts with more recent developments in peacemaking. The majority of my attention in this chapter is given to exploring the possibilities for conflict intervention using the concept of single identity work as a process that enhances the potential for collaboration among youth involved in entrenched and even intractable conflicts, especially when used in conjunction with contact-based interventions.

Assumptions about reducing intergroup conflict

Several assumptions about the reduction of intergroup conflict guided the initial design of the South Africa project that my colleagues and I developed for the U.S. Information Agency (USIA). Like many other scholar-practitioners working to reduce prejudice and intergroup conflict, we were guided by contact theory and social identity theory.

Contact theory

Since the end of World War II, social scientists have been concerned with how to reduce conflicts between groups, particularly when those conflicts are caused or heightened by identity-based differences. As Thomas Pettigrew and Linda Tropp report, the human relations movement in the late 1940s began experimenting with the use of strategic intergroup contact to reduce discrimination and prejudice.[3] Less than ten years later, Gordon Allport published his groundbreaking work, *The Nature of Prejudice*, in which he outlined the basic assumptions of contact theory.[4]

For fifty years, Allport's theory has been used as the basis for conflict interventions. During that time, researchers and practitioners have asked, "Under what conditions will contact reduce intergroup hostility?" From the beginning, there was an appreciation that contact alone was not sufficient. Allport's work began by specifying four conditions necessary for contact to have the desired effect:

1. Supportive environment. There should be institutional and social support for the intergroup contact. If social institutions are resistant to the contact or if significant identity groups are not supportive, the contact will have little positive effect.

2. Equal status. There needs to be equal status between the groups. Contact between minority and majority groups is not likely to be successful in reducing hostility unless power balancing between the groups happens first. In fact, contact between power-imbalanced groups can create the opposite effect from that desired.

3. Close contact. In order for the contact to make a difference, it must be close, prolonged, and frequent. In other words, members of the groups have to spend considerable time together over a series of interactions.

4. Cooperation. The interaction of group members must be in an environment of cooperation, not competition. This factor is later echoed in the work of Morton Deutsch, who suggested that cooperative social climates are key to developing constructive and functional conflict processes.[5]

Over the years, research has confirmed that all of these conditions are likely to reduce prejudice and the destructive intergroup conflict associated with discrimination. For example, Pettigrew and Tropp conducted a massive meta-analysis of 203 studies on intergroup contact as an influence on prejudice. Ninety-four percent of these studies found that when contact occurred under these conditions, prejudice was significantly reduced. They also found that the positive impacts applied beyond the groups in conflict. The prejudice reduction in one situation tended to extend to other situations. This is a very hopeful finding, suggesting that youth who become less prejudiced as a result of intergroup contact in one situation are likely to be less prejudiced in general and less likely to develop prejudices when encountering others who are different from them.

This effect is not the same for members of majority and minority groups, however. One cautionary note in Pettigrew and Tropp's analysis was that intergroup contact was much more likely to have the hoped-for effects with members of the majority group. For members of the minority group, the impacts were significantly less evident.[6] Practitioners working with youth from minority groups should realize that additional intervention is probably going to be necessary.

Susan Fiske and her colleagues found an important condition for contact to work. Fiske was interested in why someone would be motivated to work with another whom he or she disliked or disrespected. She argued that in order for contact to make a positive difference, the people involved had to believe that they needed each other in order to achieve some task or goal that was important to them; they had to feel they were socially interdependent. Her research on social interdependence provided support for her assumptions and demonstrated that contact without social interdependence was unlikely to make much difference in the degree of prejudice or discrimination.[7]

Social identity theory

Social science research on prejudice has followed two major theoretical perspectives: contact theory and social identity theory. Contact theory is concerned with how to structure intergroup contact to reduce discrimination, but it does not explain why these intergroup differences exist in the first place.

Social identity theory provides an explanation for why we see our membership in groups as important and why those group loyalties are likely to lead to conflict with people who are not in our group. Social identity theory rests on two premises. First, people see the world in terms of categories in such a way that they minimize the differences between people in the same category and accentuate the differences between categories. Second, since people are members of some categories and not others, there is an in-group/out-group distinction. More important, people gain a sense of identity and an emotional comfort from their membership in the group.[8]

The more we define ourselves in terms of these categories or in-groups, the more we feel the need to defend them against "outsiders." And this need is especially pronounced in adolescence, when the primary life challenge is one of forming and maintaining a social identity.[9]

What do we know about how to counteract our tendency to categorize ourselves and others? Stuart Oskamp has a fairly pessimistic assessment of how much energy we have devoted to this question:

As far back as the 1920s, prejudice has been a major topic of study in the social sciences. In fact, it is one of the most studied areas in all of psychology and sociology. However, most of the research has been aimed at describing the nature of prejudice and understanding its causes, and also, to some extent, at documenting its consequences in people's lives. Probably almost all the researchers wanted to attack prejudice and destroy its pernicious effects, but few of them have concentrated their research energies on the key question of how to reduce prejudice and create a society where equality and social justice are the norm instead of the exception.[10]

John Dovidio agrees that we have posed more possibilities than we have produced processes to accomplish these goals. He and his colleagues explain four models of intervention that can be used to decrease categorization and reduce discrimination: decategorization, recategorization, mutual differentiation, and dual identification:[11]

• Decategorization models. These models involve personal contact between members of different social groups. This is a typical outgrowth of contact hypothesis assumptions. Basically, the members of various in-groups are taken out of their groups and put together in social situations for certain periods of time. This contact leads to a breakdown of the stereotype used against the out-group. Once those barriers have lessened and people see each other as individuals, they are less likely to use the group categories to define others.

• Recategorization. This model involves uniting the people in a common in-group identity that may be new or may already exist. The hope is that the new group identity will be more important than the old identities—for example, taking "Virginians" and "Georgians" in eighteenth-century America and getting them to see themselves as "Americans." Benjamin Broome has talked about this idea as creating a "third culture." Drawing on his experience in the Greek and Turkish Cypriot conflict, he describes the power of creating a third culture with which members of two conflicting cultural groups can identify.[12]

• Mutual differentiation. This model keeps the original social groups and their differences, but sets the groups up to have to work together on some project. For example, I may not attempt to change your mind about the other group or encourage you to see yourselves as more similar, but I will ask you to work together toward the common completion of some goal that we all feel is worthwhile.

• Dual identification. In this last model, a new idea that Dovidio and his colleagues developed, people are encouraged to see themselves as members of both their original groups and a new group. In school-based conflicts with youth, there may be fights between "goths" and "geeks." These original groups do not get along. But imagine a third, overarching group identification: "conflict managers" where it is possible to be a goth and a conflict manager or a geek and a conflict manager.

Contact theory and social identity theory offer insights about what to do in a project that brings together people from various cultural and ethnic groups that had traditionally been in serious conflict. Such was the case in the mid-1990s when our team of educators began work on the Community Peace and Safety Networks project in South Africa.

Community Peace and Safety Networks in Johannesburg

If people cannot collaboratively resolve differences, democracies, and especially new democracies, are in jeopardy. Such was the case in 1995, a year after Nelson Mandela had been elected to the presidency of South Africa, a year after the de Klerk government had resigned, ending one of the most dramatic social conflicts of the twentieth century.

It was clearly a period of important and rapid social change for South Africa. The country was in the process of racially integrating institutions that had been completely segregated and unequal for some time. A critical social institution, then and now, was the educational system—the public schools. Our project involved establishing Community Peace and Safety Networks that linked school-based mediation programs and community mediation programs in four sections of Johannesburg.

Community Peace and Safety Networks (CPSN) originated in the Philadelphia region and were used to extend the impact of school-based mediation programs by involving the school, a community conflict management organization, and community members (sometimes involving police, clergy, business owners, or representatives of other community groups based in and dedicated to the neighborhood surrounding the school). The school-based and community-based mediation programs taught children constructive and collaborative approaches to handling conflicts, especially conflicts related to bias, prejudice, and discomfort with cultural diversity.

There were several reasons for the emphasis on school-based conflict programs and conflict education for youth in South Africa. The damage that had been done in the apartheid era struck most devastatingly at the youth of the country. Especially in the townships, children had been raised on a diet of violence.[13] Straker, Mendelsohn, and Tudin studied the perceptions of violence among South African youth in the apartheid and postapartheid periods and found that black-on-black violence did not decrease after the repeal of apartheid; it changed from politically motivated violence to domestic violence and random violence.[14] The township youth increasingly perceived distrust and hostility in the townships. Peace education efforts were seen as opportunities to reverse these conditions. Valerie Dovey stated that the youth "are far more assertive and 'verbal' than their parents . . . , but they are often insufficiently equipped to channel their idealism constructively. They need to have opportunities to understand, question, and challenge how society operates and how they can influence peaceful change in a positive way."[15]

After apartheid, schools were seen as an agent of social reform. The Department of Education in South Africa was very explicit about this, as Clive Harver notes in his analysis of peace education programs in South Africa:

In South Africa, government policy since 1994 has strongly emphasized education for peace and democracy. The Department of Education White Paper on Education and Training stated, "The education system must counter the legacy of violence by promoting the values underlying democratic processes and the charter of fundamental rights, the importance of due process of law and exercise of civic responsibility and by teaching the values and skills for conflict management and conflict resolution, the importance of mediation and the benefits of tolerance and cooperation.[16]

Given the changes in educational policy in postapartheid South Africa, schools were becoming more quickly integrated than other institutions. Thus, it was assumed that the educational institutions could teach and model social justice, especially given the success of conflict education in some schools.[17] These programs could build social and life skills, particularly for students in the black townships.[18] Peace and conflict education was a means of strengthening the society to more effectively manage the issues of diversity inherent in the new social configuration. These goals resonated with similar ideologies in the use of peace education for social justice in the United States.[19] And, not unimportant, conflict education programs, like those in this project, have proven effective in increasing social and emotional competencies related to constructive conflict, tolerance, and social justice.[20]

The Community Peace and Safety Networks generally were meant to build cultural bridges in two ways: (1) helping members of diverse cultural groups from South Africa to work together as a team of conflict managers who promote and deliver mediation programs and (2) encouraging South African students, teachers, and community members to collaborate in community outreach activities to increase cultural awareness and promote effective conflict management. The South African team included members from two black African townships (Soweto and Thokoza), an Afrikaans community, and a British community, as well as representatives from a black South African nongovernmental organization. In each community, a school-based conflict education and mediation program was created in a local high school and linked with a community mediation center created in that community. The project took place between 1995 and 1998.

Inadvertent but advantageous limitations on contact for youth

We originally designed activities, especially those for educators and community members, to maximize intergroup contact. We tried to create a cooperative environment and encourage a superordinate goal that required group members to work together. Based on our knowledge of contact theory research, we tried to have as much contact between the adults as possible. Interestingly, the contact, even under optimal conditions, created more tensions than it reduced. The reasons for those dynamics have been considered elsewhere.[21]

With the students, we tried to have more intergroup contact, but were limited in what we could do given unanticipated logistical and political constraints. In hindsight, it would be nice to pretend that we had planned what ended up happening, but the truth is not so friendly. While we were in the process of the project, we feared that the inadvertent limitations on student intergroup contact would severely damage the project. To our surprise, this reduced intergroup contact was quite advantageous.

Here I identify two of the inadvertent restrictions on contact. And for each, I examine the benefits we enjoyed—benefits that have led to an appreciation of the potential of single identity work.

In the beginning of the project, we had anticipated doing facilitated dialogues with students from the four high schools. In these dialogues, we hoped to gather information about their perception of the current level of conflicts and gauge the degree of intergroup tension. But due to travel restrictions, it became clear that we did not have the support of the school administrations to bring all the students together in this way. The alternative was to conduct independent focus group interviews with students from each school. In these interviews, which were conducted in the initial phases of the project and prior to mediation training, we learned about the conflict context and their preferred modes of conflict management.[22]

The focus group interviews allowed students to talk openly about their views of conflicts, something they had not done before and something they would not have done in front of students from other schools (as they later indicated in exit evaluations). They reflected on their usual approaches to managing conflicts and the extent to which those orientations were adaptable to the conflict processes emphasized in the project.

The second inadvertent reduction of contact concerned the delivery of peer mediation training to students. We saw a great opportunity for intergroup contact through mixed participation in the mediation training. We envisioned the eighty-four students from the four high schools together for four consecutive days of training. But logistics and politics intervened again. The consequence was that two mediation training sessions were held: one with the students from the township schools and the second with the students from the British and Afrikaans school.

At the time, this was a great disappointment and caused considerable stress in the project team. We felt the "separate but equal" tone of the training would communicate insincerity about collaborating across communities. And although there are elements of truth there, the reality again was that this situation ended up being better for the students and the ultimate accomplishment of project goals.

We underestimated the need for students to embrace these new ideas in an environment of safety. It was a huge change for the South African students from all communities to be empowered with the kinds of responsibilities inherent in the mediation programs we were establishing. By learning these new skills in groups they were already comfortable with, they were able to take risks and make challenges more easily. They were also able to concentrate on building relationships across similar communities, where such relationships had not existed for the youth. Prior to the project, the youth from various communities lived in a fairly isolated manner, rarely socializing outside their original community. And they had the opportunity to talk about how they saw these programs fitting in their schools and in their communities, a more tailored consideration than would have been possible in the more inclusive original design. The separate mediation trainings allowed the students opportunities for reflection, debate, and adjustment that gave them ownership they would likely not have had without it.

The students did come together across schools and had the opportunity to interact in a variety of ways during the last two stages of the project. The schools hosted mediators from all other schools in "mediation days" and meetings where the students could talk about the nature of their school mediation programs and how these were linking with the larger community. Toward the end of the project, the students helped plan and participated in a conference held for people from all four communities. These opportunities for intergroup contact, following the limitations on the same, yielded great rewards, as the following recollection suggests:

At the end of the USIA project we had a full day "conference" with all the adult and student members of the project as well as members of their communities who had not been directly involved. During the afternoon of the conference we facilitated a visioning workshop as a means of having them talk about the very long-term goals for continued action (we asked them to imagine the South Africa of 2050 and to talk about what it would be like in their ideal and what it would take to get there). At the request of the students we had two groups—an adult group and a high school student group. Both groups were very multicultural. And in both groups the majority of members had not worked together before.

At the end of the afternoon, each group was going to present their "visions" and "action lines" to the other group. Two hours passed and the adult group had not progressed at all. They were complaining that this was impossible, that there were too many pragmatics to consider, and so on and so forth. They actually started talking about how to help the students face the disappointment (assuming that the students were as blocked as they were). The students came in and asked whether we were ready to see what they had come up with. They proceeded to unfurl a huge banner on which they had developed a 50-year timeline of action leading to a well-articulated future reality. Literally, in two hours, they had created a future that they could articulate, critique, modify, and bond together about. The adults were stunned, truly speechless, in genuine awe.[23]

An introduction to single identity work

Single identity work was a concept unrecognized, or at least unpublished, when we were conducting our project. Yet it has developed and proven useful in other intractable conflict situations, most notably Northern Ireland.[24] A major impetus for single identity work was the growing dissatisfaction with contact theory interventions that were exacerbating rather than relieving the cultural tensions in Northern Ireland.[25] As Church and her colleagues state, "In many cases, contact initiatives have been found unreliable and even detrimental to community relations by reinforcing stereotypes and distrust between groups."[26]

Single identity work is a concept rather than a process, and it may take a variety of forms. The idea is that it is important to make space for interaction between members of the same group or community (usually but not exclusively defined by cultural, political, or religious identity divisions) in order for them to reflect on, think through, and critique current and future situations. The Community Relations Council of Northern Ireland describes single identity work as "projects and initiatives which provide opportunities for a single tradition to reflect on and address issues of concern. It seeks to create opportunities for a single tradition to debate complex issues relating to the conflict and to enable exploration of their own culture as part of a process. Single identity work seeks to lead to an increased awareness, understanding, respect, acknowledgement, tolerance, and active participation in the development of a pluralist society."[27]

Single identity work offers an opportunity to unearth differences that often exist between members of the same in-group. While we are tempted to assume that everyone in our group thinks as we do, we know that is not the case.[28] There are advantages to recognizing the variety of views, doing one's own "identity work" before engaging with other groups.

Single identity work can be used alone or in conjunction with intergroup contact or cross-community contact. Projects range from those that pursue "own culture validation" to those engaging in "respect for diversity" work. "Own culture validation" projects argue that single identity work is useful in its own right. "Respect for diversity" work aims to bring participants to the stage where they are able to engage with the other community. Many "respect for diversity" projects involve concurrent single identity and cross-community relations work, considering single identity work essential as both a prerequisite of and parallel to cross-community contact.[29]

There are concerns that single identity work may have negative consequences. There is the possibility that prejudices may be reinforced rather than reduced, or that attempts to promote cross-community collaboration are undermined for political or personal reasons. But these concerns are manageable and do not seem sufficient to disregard the potential of single identity work as an important resource.

Extensions of single identity work

Our experience in the South Africa project has convinced me of the power of "respect for diversity" approaches to single identity work. And although we did not have the opportunity to enact the following extensions of this idea, I offer them for consideration. How might single identity work be best used to reduce hostility among youth groups? I suggest they offer a valuable preparation to dialogue processes and a means of emotional coping for targets of contempt (usually minority and disempowered groups).

Preparation for dialogue

Dialogue is a potent process and has contributed significantly to our ability to construct the defenses of peace. As Stephen Littlejohn explains from his experience as founder of and consultant to the Transcendent Communication Project, dialogue differs from conventional interaction in a variety of ways, most notably, in terms of focus on first-order or second-order change. Conventional discussion and debate concentrates on first-order change, or changing a participant's point of view about the content being discussed. Second-order change concerns transformation of the relationship between the parties or transformation of the social system of which they are a part.[30] The goal of dialogue is a deeper understanding of self and other in order to redefine the relationship between them.

Harold Saunders recently reflected on dialogue processes in Tajikistan that he has been involved with since 1993. He summarized the five-stage model common to most dialogue processes:

Stage 1: People on different sides of a conflict decide, independently or with the encouragement of a third party, to reach out and explore peace.

Stage 2: The people come together and talk, beginning with venting and issue identification but ending with resolution to continue with more serious talks.

Stage 3: There are disciplined exchanges, with participants looking at specific problems. These exchanges are usually facilitated by a professional.

Stage 4: The parties design a scenario of interacting steps to be taken in the political arena to alter relationships.

Stage 5: The parties think of ways to put that scenario in the hands of those who can act on it.

Saunders emphasized that the focus is on transforming relationships through these five stages: "In this process of sustained dialogue there is always a dual focus: Participants, of course, focus on concrete grievances and issues, but always the moderators and participants are searching for the dynamics of the relationships that cause the problems and must be changed before the problems can be resolved."[31]

How often are people ready to take part in dialogue processes, especially with others whom they feel contempt for or who feel contempt for them? This is a quandary that has concerned me for some time but was heightened by some of the dynamics I witnessed among adult members of the South Africa project and later wrote about:

It seems that dialogue models make certain assumptions that limit their utility for the kinds of problems I have been discussing. Specifically, dialogue models focus on bringing people from relatively well-defined positions (e.g., pro-life, pro-choice) who have already identified as a member of that group to have dialogue with others from the "other side". These processes assume: (1) that participants are willing to dialogue, (2) that they are willing to communicate respectfully in the facilitated process, (3) that they have the skills to communicate respectfully (e.g., to listen, to articulate without verbal aggression), and (4) depending on the dialogue model, are willing to share personal experiences that inform the other about their individual orientation to the issues from their life experience. In my experience these are significant (and often incorrect) assumptions. "How do you motivate one who is contemptuous to engage in dialogue process?" And "How do you structure the process so that their participation will be honest rather than manipulative?"[32]

I believe that single identity work offers a possible answer to these questions. Single identity work allows us to sense the degree of contempt, confusion, or concern within a group and adjust our work accordingly. It enables us to consider whether bolstering or emotional coping may be helpful. And it presents an opportunity for members of the group to appreciate the range of viewpoints within their own group, and possibly recognize that the viewpoints of others, even those outside the group, may be worthy of respect. It also offers participants an opportunity to have a safe dialogue about uncomfortable issues before interacting with members of the out-group.

One possible template for these kinds of discussions in single identity work has been presented by Mary Alice Speke Ferdig. Without trying to be comprehensive, she suggests several examples of questions that can help change people's perspectives of other members of their group:

To focus on identity—Who am I? What is important to me? Who are we together? What do we both care about? What does each of us bring to this conversation based on our previous experiences around the topic that brings us together?

To focus on principles—What do I stand for? What do we jointly stand for? How do our choices and actions reflect our individual and collective values? How do we want to interact with one another in the context of this self-organizing process of change? What might that process look like? What can we agree on?

To focus on intentions—Where am I going? What do I want to see happen here? What are we up to in this conversation? What can we create together that brings us to where we want to be?

To focus on assumptions—What aren't we thinking about here? What is our logic for these conclusions?

To focus on exploration of possibility—What are the things you value most about yourself and the self-organizing experience of which you are a part? What are the core factors that give life and energy to the self-organizing process of which you are a part? What are the possibilities of that which we can create together based on the best of who we are?[33]

W. Barnett Pearce and Stephen Littlejohn characterize a party enjoined in moral conflict as "compelled by its highest and best motives to act in ways that are repugnant to the other [party]."[34] The more entrenched the conflict is and the more contemptuous the groups are, the more some preparatory process like single identity work may benefit. Single identity work increases the possibility that participants can "risk being changed."[35] The more secure the parties are, the more they may be willing and ready to engage in what Hill refers to as a conversation of respect: "Conversations of respect . . . are ones in which the participants expect to learn from each other, expect to learn non-incidental things, expect to change at least intellectually as a result of the encounter."[36]

I have framed this use of single identity work in terms of preparation for dialogue as a means of intergroup contact. But in situations where "own culture validation" is the goal, the same processes can produce conversations of respect within the youth group as well.

Emotional coping

Pettigrew and Tropp believed that intergroup contact often had different effects on members of majority groups as compared with members of minority groups. I believe that a plausible explanation for this is that members of minority groups have had to endure often intense, unrelenting, and devastating emotional damage as targets of the contempt of members of the majority. Even when attacks against their group have not been directed at them personally, youth targeted by the attacks may suffer damage to self-esteem and may doubt their ability to respond effectively to the attacks.[37] As social identity theory argues, once a person has categorized herself as a member of a social group, she bases an aspect of her self-esteem (collective self-esteem) on the perceived value of that group.[38] Damage to the group identity results in loss of personal face.

An exciting application of single identity work is helping members of minority groups cope emotionally as a means of empowering them for intergroup contact. Support from this idea comes from research on prejudice reduction and on adolescent identity and self-esteem.

Brenda Major and her colleagues raise an important question: "What can a target of prejudice do to lessen the impact of prejudice?" They note that this question has received very little attention in the volumes of literature written on prejudice and discrimination. The answer they propose is to teach targets of prejudice emotional coping strategies. Using Robert Lazarus's theory of emotional appraisal and reappraisal, Major suggests two strategies: emotion-focused coping and problem-focused coping. The former involves teaching yourself to reappraise the situation that led to your emotional experience—in other words, to help yourself feel better about the situation by altering your perception of the attacker or your ability to deal with the problem. This leads to work on problem-focused coping or how to prevent the prejudiced person from attacking you (perhaps by reducing her prejudiced attitudes toward you, limiting her access to you, or developing alliances with more powerful others).[39]

But emotional coping cannot take place in a public situation, and certainly not in front of conflicting parties. It requires a facilitated conversation in a private and safe space. Thus, single identity work provides a context that allows youth to identify times and ways they have been disrespected, how they have felt about that, and how they might be able to cope through reappraisal. Similar processes using Lazarus's model have been applied to other conflict contexts.[40]

One reason that emotional coping with contempt requires safety is that the contemptuous behavior usually creates a sense of shame that makes the target vulnerable to the attacker. Michael Lewis argues that the link between contempt and shame can be very important for group and interpersonal conflict, especially among adolescents.[41] Does being treated with contempt cause shame? It may, if we accept the evaluation of others and use it as a mirror by which we see ourselves. If being treated contemptuously results in shame, it may result in the shame reparation cycles discussed in detail by Suzanne Retzinger.[42] She argues that someone who has been shamed usually makes some sign that this has happened. Through verbal or nonverbal communication, the person "announces" that she is feeling ashamed and "demands" that the person who hurt her do something to make the situation right. In healthy relationships, the response is usually a quick attempt by the offending person at repair. But in relationships where one party feels openly contemptuous of the other, repair is very unlikely. In fact, the attacker may even be motivated to use harsher forms of behavior.

The attacker is usually tempted to continue the contemptuous behavior because contempt is a self-perpetuating emotion; it is seductive. This dynamic is evident among youth groups where insults are hurled until they have done damage. Like blood to sharks, the sense of hitting the mark often stimulates more of the same behavior, which escalates the conflict.

Fortunately, there is some evidence that focusing on strengths of a culture or ethnic identity can increase self-esteem and reduce the ability of the other's contempt to harm you or leave you feeling ashamed and unprotected. Recent research on ethnic immersion, a process similar to single identity work but more general in scope, suggests that attention and reflection on one's group identity can bolster self-esteem, especially for adolescents.[43]

If single identity work is a mechanism for emotional coping, especially for minority youth, we still need a lot of work on techniques for accomplishing these ends. What is the best way to facilitate such sessions? How private should these be? What are the benefits of having emotional coping be a group interaction, especially in cultures that have a more collective rather than individual sense of self? Appreciating the possibilities of single identity work opens the door to pressing questions about its form and delivery.

Conclusion

I believe, as the UNESCO Preamble states, that wars do indeed begin in the minds of men. And I believe, like Carol Izard, that contempt is the pernicious emotion that gives rise to thoughts of physical and psychological violence against an other:

In contempt, one feels prejudiced against some object, idea or person . . . contempt may have emerged as a vehicle for preparing the individual or group to face a dangerous adversary. For example, a young man might prepare for defense of himself or of his group with such thoughts as: "I am stronger than he, I am better." Eventually, this message might become a rallying signal for all the men in preparation for defense or attack. Perhaps those who were quite persuaded marshaled more courage (and felt less empathy for the enemy) and were more successful in surviving the hazards of hunting and fighting. Still today the occasions that elicit contempt are situations in which one needs to feel stronger, more intelligent, more civilized, or in some way better than, the person one is contending with. . . . However, once contempt is turned against other human beings, it is hard to find anything positive or adaptive in this emotion.[44]

To the extent that we can decrease the tendency of youth to have contempt for others or to let others' displays of contempt affect them, we may have sown seeds of the defenses of peace. While intergroup contact under certain conditions can reduce prejudice fueled by contempt, there are possibilities for single identity work to contribute to this process as a preparation for intergroup contact or as a replacement for it. As conflict practitioners, we are only at the beginning of our discussion about these important possibilities. We can hope that one day, as the South Africans might say, we will see these ideas contribute to *Thokoza* (peace) in our lifetime.

Notes

1. Harris, I. M., & Morrison, M. L. (2003). *Peace education* (2nd ed.). Jefferson, NC: McFarland.

2. Jones, T. S. (1998). *Final report: Community Peace and Safety Networks: Linking community and school-based mediation in South Africa.* Washington, DC: U.S. Information Agency, Office of Citizen Exchanges Bureau of Educational and Cultural Affairs.

3. Pettigrew, T. F., & Tropp, L. R. (2000). Does intergroup contact reduce prejudice? Recent meta-analytic findings. In S. Oskamp (Ed.), *Reducing prejudice and discrimination* (pp. 93–114). Mahwah, NJ: Erlbaum.

4. Tal-Or, N., Boninger, D., & Gleicher, F. (2000). Understanding the conditions and processes necessary for intergroup contact to reduce prejudice. In S. Oskamp (Ed.), *Reducing prejudice and discrimination* (pp. 89–107). Mahwah, NJ: Erlbaum. See also Allport, G. W. (1954). *The nature of prejudice.* Reading, MA: Addison-Wesley. For a thorough history of contact theory and the research conducted on contact hypotheses, see Pettigrew, T. F. (1998). Intergroup contact theory. *Annual Review of Psychology, 49,* 65–85.

5. Deutsch, M. (1973). *The resolution of conflict.* New Haven, CT: Yale University Press.

6. Pettigrew & Tropp. (2000).

7. Fiske, S. T. (2000). Interdependence and the reduction of prejudice. In S. Oskamp (Ed.), *Reducing prejudice and discrimination* (pp. 115–135). Mahwah, NJ: Erlbaum.

8. Brewer, M. B. (2000). Reducing prejudice through cross-categorization: Effects of multiple social identities. In S. Oskamp (Ed.), *Reducing prejudice and discrimination* (pp. 165–184). Mahwah, NJ: Erlbaum. Luhtanen, R., & Crocker, J. (1992). A collective self-esteem scale: Self-evaluation of one's societal identity. *Personality and Social Psychology Bulletin, 18,* 302–218. Tajfel, H., & Turner, J. C. (1986). The social identity theory of intergroup behavior. In S. Worchel & W. G. Austin (Eds.), *Psychology of intergroup relations* (pp. 7–12). Chicago: Nelson Hall.

9. Erikson, E. (1968). *Identity: Youth and crisis.* New York: Norton. Gergen, K. (1991). *The saturated self: Dilemmas of identity in contemporary life.* New York: Basic Books. Giddens, A. (1991). *Modernity and self-identity: Self and society in the late modern age.* Cambridge, MA: Polity Press.

10. Oskamp, S. (Ed.), *Reducing prejudice and discrimination.* Mahwah, NJ: Erlbaum.

11. Dovidio, J. F., Kawakami, K., & Gaertner, S. L. (2000). Reducing contemporary prejudice: Bias at the individual and group level. In S. Oskamp (Ed.), *Reducing prejudice and discrimination* (pp. 137–164). Mahwah, NJ: Erlbaum.

12. Allen, B., Broome, B., Jones, T., Chen, V., & Collier, M.-J. (2003). Intercultural alliances: A cyberdialogue among scholar practitioners. In M. Collier (Ed.), *Intercultural alliances: Critical transformation* (pp. 279–319). Thousand Oaks, CA: Sage.

13. Fourie, E. (1990). The UN Convention on the Rights of the Child and the crisis for children in South Africa: Apartheid and detention. *Human Rights Quarterly, 12,* 106–114. See also Gibson, K. (1989). Children in political violence. *Social Science and Medicine, 28,* 659–667. Swartz, L., & Levett, A. (1989). Political repression and children in South Africa: The social construction of damaging effects. *Social Science and Medicine, 28,* 741–750.

14. Straker, G., Mendelsohn, F. M., & Tudin, P. (1996). Violent political contexts and the emotional concerns of township youth. *Child Development, 67,* 46–54.

15. Dovey, V. (1994). *Exploring peace education in South African settings.* Malmo, Sweden: School of Education. (ERIC Document Reproduction Service No. ED 384 542)

16. Harver, C. (2003). Safe schools: Violence and the struggle for peace and democracy in South African education. In E. E. Uwazie (Ed.), *Conflict resolution and peace education in Africa* (pp. 77–87). San Francisco: New Lexington Press.

17. Connell, R. W. (1993). *Schools and social justice.* Philadelphia: Temple University Press. Dovey (1994). See also Tihanyi, K. Z., & du Toit, F. (in press). Reconciliation through integration? An examination of South Africa's reconciliation process in racially integrating high schools, *Conflict Resolution Quarterly.* Tihanyi and du Toit detail the extent of the educational reforms associated with the end of apartheid, including the centralization of a previously (racially) divided education administration, the introduction of new curricula, and the racial desegregation of the schools. However, they point out that racial desegregation has been limited to only a small subset of schools, even in 2004.

18. Akanda, A. (1995). Communication—its effect on the self-concept of children: A South African perspective. *Early Childhood Development and Care, 105,* 69–76. Macdonald, C. A. (1990). *Crossing the threshold into standard three in black education: The consolidated main report of the Threshold project.* Pretoria: Human Sciences Research Council. (ERIC Document Reproduction Service No. ED 344 469) Stead, G. B. (1996). Career development of black South African adolescents: A developmental-contextual perspective. *Journal of Counseling and Development, 74,* 270–275.

19. Bettman, E. H., & Moore, P. (1994). Conflict resolution programs and social justice. *Education and Urban Society, 27,* 11–21. Girard, K., & Koch, S. J. (1996). *Conflict resolution in the schools: A manual for educators.* San Francisco: Jossey-Bass. Salomon, G., & Nevo, B. (2002). *Peace education: The concept, principles and practices around the world.* Mahwah, NJ: Erlbaum. Townley, A. (1994). Conflict resolution, diversity, and social justice. *Education and Urban Society, 27,* 5–10.

20. Jones, T. S. (in press). Conflict resolution education: Research proven practices. In J. Oetzel & S. Ting-Toomey (Eds.), *Handbook of communication and conflict.* Thousand Oaks, CA: Sage. Jones, T. S., & Compton, R. O. (Eds.).

(2003). *Kids working it out: Stories and strategies for making peace in our schools.* San Francisco: Jossey-Bass. Jones, T. S., & Kmitta, D. (2000). *Does it work? The case for conflict resolution education in our nation's schools.* Washington, DC: CRENet/Association for Conflict Resolution.

21. Jones, T. S., & Bodtker, A. (1998). A dialectical analysis of a social justice process: International collaboration in South Africa. *Journal of Applied Communication Research, 26,* 357–373. See also Allen et al. (2003).

22. The types of conflicts reported by the South African students resemble those conflicts reported by students in U.S. schools (for example, rumors, he said/she said, boyfriend-girlfriend disputes, disobeying rules, and arguments with teachers). Racial conflict was also reported, primarily by students in the predominantly white schools, but was not posed as intractable. Language was seen as an important cultural cue tied to conflict (for example, which language gets privileged in interaction) and was also a source of misunderstanding between students.

The greatest diversity between the student groups was in how they managed conflicts. The British students relied on authority to manage conflicts between peers. Students also reported the use of direct confrontation, yet ensuing talk typically involved attempts to persuade one another rather than genuine discussion. Thus, the conflict was often left unresolved unless it was brought to the attention of one of the supervisors.

The Afrikaans students dealt with conflict almost exclusively through peer groups and rarely consulted adults in the school to assist them. Interpersonal conflict, or conflict between members of a peer group, became a group issue, often with the "leader" of the group and other group members taking the responsibility of negotiating for the members in conflict. They also placed a high value on face saving in this context. If the issue had not been adequately addressed (that is, if the injured party did not feel redeemed), they waited until another explicit issue (related or not) arose, or they created another issue, and then went through the same process. The girls at the Afrikaans school also reported that conflicts were frequently managed through silence. Very similar patterns were discovered independently by Tihanyi and du Toit (in press). In their ethnographic analysis of racial integration in South African high schools, they found that racial and ethnic orientations to conflict and conflict management still affect the extent to which reconciliation mechanisms are at work in the South African educational system.

23. Tricia Jones, quoted in Allen et al. (2003). Pp. 300–301.

24. Church, C., Visser, A., & Johnson, L. Shepherd. (2003). A path to peace or persistence? The "single identity" approach to conflict resolution in Northern Ireland. *Conflict Resolution Quarterly, 21*(3), 1–24. Church C., & Visser, A. *Single identity work.* Derry/Londonderry, Northern Ireland: INCORE, 2001. I am indebted to Cheyenne Church and her colleagues, who refined the concept through their work with the Local International Learning Project at INCORE in 2001–2002.

25. Hewstone, M., & Brown, R. (1986). Contact is not enough: An intergroup perspective on the "contact hypothesis." In M. Hewstone & R. Brown (Eds.), *Contact and conflict in intergroup encounters.* Oxford: Basil Blackwell. Hughes, J., & Carmichael, P. (1998). Community relations in Northern Ire-

land: Attitudes to contact and integration. In G. Robinson, D. Heenan, K. Thompson, & Gray, A. M. (Eds.), *Social attitudes in Northern Ireland: The seventh report*. Aldershot: Ashgate Publishing.

26. Church et al. (2003). P. 1.

27. As presented in Church et al. (2003). They reference the quote from www.community-relations.org.uk/progs/community/community.htm.

28. Leichty, J., & Clegg, C. (2000). *Moving beyond sectarianism: Religion, conflict and reconciliation in Northern Ireland*. Dublin: Columbia Press.

29. Hughes, J., & Donnelly, C. (1998). *Single identity community relations*. Jordanstown: University of Ulster.

30. Littlejohn, S. (2003). The Transcendent Communication Project: Searching for a praxis of dialogue. *Conflict Resolution Quarterly, 21*(3), 65–83. See also Arnett, R. C., & Arneson, P. (1999). *Dialogic civility in a cynical age: Community, hope, and interpersonal relationships*. Albany, N.Y.: SUNY Press. Arnett, R. C. (1986). *Communication and community: Implications of Martin Buber's Dialogue*. Carbondale: Southern Illinois University Press.

31. Saunders, H. H. (2003). Sustained dialogue in managing intractable conflict. *Negotiation Journal, 19*(1), 85–95.

32. Jones, T. S. (2000, Mar.). *Pride and prejudice: Considering the role of contempt in community and conflict*. Paper presented at the Baylor University Conference on Practical Theory and Dialogue, Waco, TX.

33. Ferdig, M.A.S. (2001). *Exploring the social construction of complex self-organizing change: A study of emerging change in the regulation of nuclear power*. Unpublished doctoral dissertation, Benedictine University.

34. Pearce, W. B., & Littlejohn, S. (1997). *Moral conflict: When social worlds collide*. Thousand Oaks, CA: Sage. P. 7

35. Pearce & Littlejohn. (1997). P. 161.

36. As quoted in Pearce & Littlejohn. (1997). P. 161.

37. Boeckmann, R. J., & Liew, J. (2002). Hate speech: Asian American students' justice judgments and psychological responses. *Journal of Social Issues, 58*, 363–381.

38. Lawrence, C. R. III, Matsuda, M. J., Delgado, R., & Crenshaw, K. W. (1993). Introduction. In M. J. Matsuda, C. R. Lawrence, R. Delgado, & K. W. Crenshaw (Eds.), *Words that wound: Critical race theory, assaultive speech, and the First Amendment* (pp. 1–13). Boulder, CO: Westview. See also Luhtanen & Crocker. (1992). Tajfel & Turner. (1986).

39. Major, B., Quinton, W., J., McCoy, S. K., & Schmader, T. (2000). Reducing prejudice: The target's perspective. In S. Oskamp (Ed.), *Reducing prejudice and discrimination* (pp. 211–238). Mahwah, NJ: Erlbaum.

40. Jones, T. S., & Bodtker, A. (2001). Mediating with heart in mind. *Negotiation Journal, 17*, 217–244.

41. Lewis, M. (1993). Self-conscious emotions: Embarrassment, pride, shame, and guilt. In M. Lewis & J. M. Haviland (Eds.), *Handbook of emotions* (pp. 563–573). New York: Guilford Press. See also Hawley, W., & Jackson, A. (Eds.). (1995). *Toward a common destiny: Improving race and ethnic relations in America*. San Francisco: Jossey-Bass. Miller, W. I. (1997). *The anatomy of disgust*. Cambridge, MA: Harvard University Press.

42. Retzinger, S. M. (1991). Shame, anger, and conflict: Case study of emotional violence. *Journal of Family Violence, 6*, 37–59. Retzinger, S. M. (1993). *Violent emotions: Shame and rage in marital quarrels.* Thousand Oaks, CA: Sage.

43. Allen, R. L. (1994). *Group identification and self-esteem in the African-American community: I am because we are.* Unpublished manuscript. Ann Arbor, MI: University of Michigan. Corenblum, B., & Annis, R. C. (1993). Development of racial identity in minority and majority children: An affect discrepancy model. Available at: www.cpa.ca.cjbsnew/1993/october. DuBois, D. L., Burk-Braxton, C., Swenson, L. P., Tevendale, H. D., & Hardesty, J. L. (2002). Race and gender influences on adjustment in early adolescence: Investigation of an integrative model. *Child Development, 73*(5), 1573-1592.

44. Izard, C. (1977). *Human emotions.* New York: Plenum Press.

TRICIA S. JONES *is a professor in the Department of Psychological Studies at Temple University in Philadelphia, Pennsylvania.*

In the woods of Maine, young people from conflict regions meet to learn about themselves, each other, and their potential to promote peace.

2

Seeds of Peace: Toward a common narrative

Marieke van Woerkom

JOHN WALLACH HAD BEEN a journalist in the Middle East for decades. He had grown tired of sitting on the sidelines as the Arab-Israeli conflict played itself out. He wanted to effect change in more direct ways and, as he shared with the *Saudi Gazette*, "it occurred to [him] . . . to begin a programme that would change the next generation of Arabs and Israelis together. If peace is going to have a chance," he asserted, "it must begin in the hearts of both peoples when they are young."[1] For ten years, Wallach worked tirelessly to make this belief a reality until his premature death in 2002.

The Seeds of Peace program began in August 1993 when forty-eight Egyptian, Israeli, and Arabic boys met at a summer camp in Maine for a two-week coexistence program that gave them the opportunity not only to meet their "enemies" for the first time, but to live with them in cabins, share meals, and participate in typical summer camp activities. In addition, these boys were involved in daily dialogue sessions that allowed them the opportunity to discuss, analyze, and understand the experiences they and their counterparts had had as a result of their conflict, while at the same time exploring related impressions and feelings. At the end of the program,

NEW DIRECTIONS FOR YOUTH DEVELOPMENT, NO. 102, SUMMER 2004 © WILEY PERIODICALS, INC.

these forty-eight boys were invited to attend the signing of the Declaration of Principles on the White House lawn.[2]

Since that time, Seeds of Peace has brought an increasing number of youth to Maine, boys as well as girls, from a growing number of countries and conflict regions. Currently, the Middle East program includes youth participants from Egypt, Israel, Jordan, Morocco, Qatar, Tunisia, Yemen, the West Bank, and Gaza. In 1998, Seeds of Peace started a Cyprus program, adding youth from mainland Turkey and Greece in 1999. In 2000, a Balkans program was initiated, as well as one for a diverse group of youth from Maine's inner cities. In 2001, a program began for youth from India and Pakistan, and in 2002 an Afghan program was launched.[3]

Although two-thirds of the program continues to focus on the Middle East, Seeds of Peace has developed a model for coexistence that, when adapted appropriately, allows young people from a given conflict region to work on their differences collaboratively toward a transformation that promotes understanding and respect between the conflicting parties. With the right motivation and support, young people can help transform the most intractable conflicts into more productive modes of interaction. Communication and collaboration are key in this process, laying the groundwork for sustainable peace.

The baggage of war

Governments around the world employ education "to spread the image and heritage of the 'nation' and to inculcate attachment to it."[4] History and literature classes in particular are critical channels for instilling in students a standardized, state-sanctioned perception of the nation. In the classroom, heroes and enemies spring to life. Events of the past are given meaning through connection to current circumstances, or, as the case may be, they are ignored. Even while young, students learn characteristics of loyal citizenship in the classroom and develop a sense of collective identity.

This curricular narrative informs the understanding of history in many regions of the world, including the Middle East. In an article on Jewish-Arab conflict resolution in Israel, Feuerverger analyzes "classes of 'Modelet,' which is a Hebrew word meaning birthplace and is an important part of the Jewish Israeli curriculum." She explains: "The subject is also called 'yediat ha'aretz' or 'knowledge of the land' and covers geography, geology, history, ethnology, and botany."[5] *Modelet* presents a very one-sided view, however, leaving Arabs out of the picture, especially those who remained in Israel after 1948. This is also the case with the way in which the events of 1948 are generally portrayed in Jewish Israeli history books—as the "culmination of a teleological process of redemption and renaissance of the Jewish people."[6] Pappe explains that the Israeli representation of the war is constructed carefully so as to present Zionism as a Third World liberation movement. Interestingly, "the two terms used for the 1948 war do not indicate any direct conflict with the Arabs: 'independence' from the British (Azma'ut) and 'liberation' from the yoke of the Diaspora (Shirur)."[7]

The Palestinian and other Arab perceptions of Zionism are diametrically opposed to this Israeli version. In the 1968 Palestinian National Charter, Zionism was condemned specifically as "colonialist . . . in its inception, aggressive and expansionist in its goals, racist and segregationist in its configurations and fascist in its means and aims." Not surprisingly, this is often the tone also used in Palestinian classrooms when teaching Palestinians about their history—a history of oppression, a history of injustice.

Still, the various curricula in the Middle East are more than merely antithetical. In some textbooks, events are ignored or marginalized, whereas in others they hold prominent positions. Consider the Holocaust, which is central to Jewish history. Throughout their schooling, Israeli schoolchildren learn about the near-annihilation of European Jewry by the Nazis. Yet the schoolbooks of surrounding Arab states, if they mention the Holocaust at all, tend to trivialize it, describing it as a Jewish excuse for a state. This "widely divergent treatment of the Holocaust . . . is the most powerful example, but it is not the only one."[8] *Al-Nakba* ("the catastrophe"), the Palestinian displacement from their homes as a result of the 1948 war, is central to Palestinian history and is practically ignored in Israeli textbooks. In addition, Israeli and Arab youth learn opposing versions of who lived in the West Bank and Gaza when the first Zionists arrived, who attacked whom, who won which war, who is the aggressor, and who the victim.

What these youngsters are taught in their respective classrooms has very little to do with peace. Instead, it is what social psychologist Dani Bar Tal refers to as "conflict ethos." As he explains, for "conflict a society needs a psychological foundation as much as it needs weaponry and economic strength."[9] Indeed, such diverse narratives are not unique to the Arab-Israeli struggle. They exist in other conflict regions as well, as the young people discover when they arrive at camp.

Participants in the Seeds of Peace program

Youth who participate in the Seeds of Peace program do so with all sorts of emotional and psychological baggage. They come with their prejudices and fears, their experiences, life stories, and widely divergent historical accounts. Some have witnessed atrocious scenes and experienced intensely traumatic events. They have been raised within cultures of animosity, with an omnipresent conflict ethos. The Seeds of Peace International Camp in Maine creates the space for these youth to meet each other in a safe and supportive environment, where all are treated as equals.

The selection process

Thousands of young people apply each year for the limited spots available at the Seeds of Peace International Camp. Through a rigorous selection process, the organization targets those youths who are expected to have an impact on their communities when returning home—smart and confident youths who take initiative, are not afraid to take risks, and are likely to be tomorrow's leaders. In addition, Seeds of Peace seeks out those youth who speak English well enough to be able to communicate with those from the "other" side, while at camp and upon returning home.

Applicants write essays in English and are interviewed individually and in groups. In some parts of the world, governments are involved directly in the camp selection process; in other parts, there is a tacit governmental endorsement of the program. As a result, the youths who attend Seeds of Peace programs are a diverse group that ranges in political opinion and comes from various economic backgrounds.

Arrival at the camp

As the buses arrive at camp and the young people get off, many appear apprehensive, while others are quite prepared to take on their enemy. Israelis have arrived at camp wrapped in their flag, or wearing T-shirts with stars of David stretching across the front or back. Palestinians come wearing pendants, several inches in diameter, of their flags in the shape of historical Palestine, and *kaffiyahs* are wrapped around many shoulders and heads as the Palestinian delegation gets off the bus.[10]

When assigned to their cabins, the uneasiness persists at the thought of sharing a living space with those whom they "know" to be their enemy. It is generally their first time meeting and interacting with teens from the other side, and, conditioned by a profound distrust and a deep-seated prejudice, the youth often experience difficulty in seeing their bunkmates as fellow teens who are similar to them in many ways. When contrast and opposition are the primary lessons learned back home, recognizing shared humanity is difficult. This becomes clear when talking with the youth in those first days of camp and shows as delegations stick with "their kind," trying hard to stay within their comfort zone. "You know," a Greek Cypriot participant once shared, "it is not very easy to have so much trust to the other so as to sleep in the bed near her, especially when this other is a Turkish Cypriot girl."

In an extreme case, in the early years of Seeds of Peace, an Israeli boy refused to go to sleep his first night of camp for fear of not waking up the next morning. He was found wandering around camp past midnight and shared with camp staff his fear of Palestinians, whom he knew only as terrorists and killers. It was hard to convince him to go back to his bunk that night. Ironically, other campers have gone to sleep next to each other quite willingly, finding out only the next morning, as they are introduced to their enemy and bunkmate, "how much danger they were in" the night before.

Yet as the young people get involved in the summer camp's team sports, as they perform music and drama together, and as they get to know each other in their bunks and in the dining hall, it becomes possible for them to recognize that "the other side" is made up of human beings, some of whom they are able to connect with and even like as a person or friend. Important as this part of the program is, however, it is not enough. The connection needs to take hold on a deeper level if it is to last beyond the three-week camp experience. This becomes possible only when addressing the root causes of conflict head-on, through dialogue between the parties involved.

The Seeds of Peace dialogue program

Many of the youth who attend the camp are eager to discuss their situation. They want to express the anger, sadness, fear, and frustration that result from living in a context of violence and antagonism. Some want to discuss the past; others want to work on a shared vision of the future. Many are extremely passionate advocates of the truth that they have been taught. Few of the young people, however, are equipped with the skills to communicate effectively. They are more prepared to talk than listen, to blame than acknowledge responsibility, and to argue rather than think critically and constructively.

The dialogue sessions at Seeds of Peace are designed to create opportunities for the young people to discuss the harder and more contentious issues and to learn the communication skills necessary to do so in a productive and meaningful way.[11] In the process, the young people are encouraged to expand their capacity for critical reflection and deepen their understanding of each other and of the conflict that they grew up with. Trained facilitators work to create a safe environment where the young people can express their thoughts and feelings about their conflict and the many ways in which it affects their lives.[12] The dialogue process can be broken down into roughly three phases:

Phase One, during which a foundation of trust, connection and respect is established;

Phase Two, during which more substantive and, at times, contentious dialogue takes place, allowing for enhanced awareness, understanding, and empathy for the Other;

Phase Three, during which the young people are prepared for returning home to an environment of misunderstanding, discord, and violence.

The strategies used, and the degrees of structure and intervention that facilitators rely on, vary from group to group and are based for the most part on the facilitators' assessments of the needs of a particular group.

Phase One

Facilitators focus on introductions and on group and trust building during the first sessions with their groups. Using various activities, facilitators give group members a chance to learn each other's names and get to know each other on a personal level. This initial discovery process allows the young people to accustom themselves to the dialogue group environment while starting the learning process.

At the same time, elsewhere in camp, many of the participants are surprised to find out that similarities exist between them and their "enemies." Indians and Pakistanis discover that Urdu and Hindi are practically the same language and that they are able to communicate with each other using their mother tongue. Cypriots discover that although their Greek and Turkish languages are different, they nonetheless share certain words as a result of centuries of coexistence on the island. Despite recent Balkan efforts to separate the language of Serbo-Croatian into three different languages of Bosnian, Croatian, and Serbian for the three "different" peoples, this has been achieved in only limited measure, thus allowing the Balkan youths at Seeds of Peace to communicate among themselves in their own language. The use of the word *y'allah* (let's go) among both Israelis and Arabs, moreover, has been translated into the common parlance of all at camp—staff and campers alike.

Beyond linguistic discoveries, youth may find a common interest in computers, a liking of hip-hop or of certain television shows. They may be intrigued by the meaning of someone's name, or figure out that taste and fashion are not contained by borders. During one of the early sessions a few years back, two girls, one Israeli and the other Palestinian, were surprised to find that each of their families was worried about their attending the Seeds of Peace summer camp. It allowed them to see each other as part of a larger family, with parents and grandparents who experienced the same emotions.

Differences invariably come up in these early sessions. However, rather than expanding on them, facilitators use exercises that create opportunities for the youth to establish a certain level of trust. The youth need this foundation of trust to be in place before a dialogue on differences and other more contentious issues can be productive.

In addition, groups discuss and agree on guidelines, such as confidentiality, that will allow each member to feel safe. Confidentiality is a key element of the Seeds of Peace dialogue sessions.

Phase Two

Having established a foundation of trust, connection, and respect, the young people are ready to explore together some of the more contentious issues and gain a deeper understanding of the conflict and the ways in which it affects themselves and others. By this phase in the dialogue process, young people from the more heated conflict regions like the Middle East and Kosovo/a are often anxious to share their experiences of the conflict and may want to share incidents or moments that convey their fears, losses, frustrations, and humiliations. Whether it is the shelling of Palestinian civilians by the Israeli army or the effects of suicide bombers on Israeli noncombatants, the killing of Hindus fleeing to India or Muslims fleeing to Pakistan after partition, all sides have their stories, and all sides have their pain. The narratives shared at this point in the dialogue process often tell of historical or existing struggles against the malevolence of the other national group.

Usually these accounts are hard to listen to for those from the other side, and the group may need structures to be imposed that will make this exchange possible. This may mean splitting the group into smaller groups (triads or pairs) or assigning roles of who gets to speak and who gets to listen. Asking youth to paraphrase what they hear may be difficult, but it is another way to allow them to pause and think before they respond.

Difficult though this exchange may be, it is an important part of the process of conflict transformation. As an Indian camper shared after an intense dialogue session in the second week of camp, "I don't understand. Why do I hate them [the Pakistanis] so much? I don't even know them, and still I hate them." She was in tears as she spoke. The youth may have great difficulty hearing and acknowledging this controversial new information, especially when they feel they have not been heard or acknowledged themselves. For example, after one of the group's Serb participants had shared her feelings of oppression and fear of living in Kosovo/a, a Kosovar-Albanian group member responded: "I cannot hear you, because when you share your story, the volume of my own story goes up in my head. I cannot imagine your fear because I am blinded by the images of my own story that play themselves out before my eyes when you start talking." Having experienced personal trauma at the hands of the Serbs for years, she took a great step in sharing this with her counterparts so clearly, especially as she continued by saying that cracks had started to appear in her own story—cracks that were allowing her to start looking beyond her own pain.

Through a wide range of activities and through reflecting on the process of the group as it evolves, the young people learn to move beyond simply expressing their thoughts and feelings to communicating with an awareness of the sensibilities of those who are listening. At the same time, the youth expand their capacity to listen and learn to distinguish between the individual and the groups with which they identify, keeping in mind that the conflict is one between national groups, whereas the recognition and connection they are making takes place on an individual level. As a result, the discovery is made that people on all sides suffer because of the conflict. Genuine caring and compassion for group members can develop.

With a certain level of empathy and stronger communication skills in place, the youth can now start to debate their shared history more constructively, distinguishing in the end between useful acknowledgment of painful history and staying stuck in the past. Many develop the ability to simultaneously feel pride in the history and culture of their people while adopting a questioning attitude toward certain aspects of their national historical narratives and particular policies or actions of their governments. It is a confusing process that raises many questions and conflicting feelings for the young people.

As the young people start to recognize the multidimensional nature of the conflict between their communities, the facilitators invite the group members to look at how history is constructed and also to examine how the media present the news, where stereotypes stem from, and how power dynamics influence the relationships between their peoples. Facilitators may challenge the young people to consider the impact of various kinds of power on their interactions with each other and on the possibilities for a fair and just solution to the conflict in their region.

Ultimately, facilitators seek to help participants move beyond defending readily held positions toward the consideration of the details of a shared vision of the future. On certain issues, young people may agree to disagree, which in itself can be an accomplishment, as long as the different perspectives have been heard and are recognized by the various members of the group. For example, Israelis may remain convinced that their security is improved through checkpoints while learning through dialogue about the damage inflicted on Palestinian society. In the same dialogue, Palestinians can come to understand the Israeli fear of suicide bombers, even if this fear does not justify the imposition of checkpoints. Although the issue remains unresolved, both sides have learned to understand the other better.

Phase Three

In the final dialogue sessions, the facilitators make sure to prepare the young people for going back home. Having let down their guard and opened themselves up to new insights, perspectives, and ideas, the participants need to recognize that not everyone back home will be willing to hear what they have to say. Leaving the safe camp environment will present the young people with their biggest challenge yet: facing their families and friends, their teachers, fellow students, and others who may have quite different, more rigid opinions and views of the conflict and of those on the other side of it. For some youth, going home will mean facing the immediate dangers of war, and they will need to have their defenses up before heading back out.

Returning home

Commonly, when youth return home, they are accused of being traitors. In many of their countries, engaging with the "enemy" in any way, let alone building relationships of understanding, is simply unacceptable. For this reason, Seeds of Peace continues its programming in the regions that the youth are from, providing them with support, encouragement, and continued programming that challenges and inspires them. Indeed, the Seeds of Peace summer camp, extensive though it is, is merely a jumping-off point that fits into a much wider scheme of programming: a conflict transformation and leadership track that takes place over the course of participants' young adult lives as they come into their own and create a community based on a new collective identity—that of a Seed of Peace.

Notes

1. Ferguson, B. (1995, Oct. 30). Seeds of Peace dissolves friction into friendship. *Saudi (Jeddah, Saudi Arabia) Gazette*, 17.

2. The Declaration of Principles on Interim Self-Government Arrangements, informally known as the Oslo Accords or Oslo Peace Accords, was a series of agreements between the Israeli government and the Palestine Liberation Organization in 1993 as part of a peace process between the two parties.

3. The Afghan program at Seeds of Peace is slightly different from the other programs that the organization conducts. Afghan youth do participate in camp life in the same way that youth from other conflict regions do, learning about nonviolent interaction in the process. Yet in their dialogue sessions, the Afghan

participants deal more with internal issues than with an outside enemy. The youth are given the opportunity to share their stories of oppression and violence with one another and with a small group of Americans that joins them in their sessions. In this way, a cultural exchange becomes possible, and the Afghan youth are not isolated in the same way that Afghanistan had been isolated from the rest of the world for the decades preceding the fall of the Taliban.

4. Hobsbawn, E. J. (1990). *Nations and nationalism since 1780: Programme, myth, reality* (new and rev. ed.). Cambridge: Cambridge University Press. P. 91.

5. Feuerverger, G. (1997). An educational program for peace: Jewish-Arab conflict resolution in Israel. *Theory and Practice, 36*, 17–24.

6. Pappe, I. (1997). Post Zionist critique on Israel and the Palestinians, part 1: The academic debate. *Journal of Palestine Studies, 26*, 29–44.

7. Pappe. (1997).

8. Sachs, S. (1995, Oct. 22). Reading, writing and hate: As Israeli, Arab leaders make peace, schoolchildren still learn lessons of war. *Newsday*, p. A7.

9. Bar-tal, D. (2000). From intractable conflict through conflict resolution to reconciliation: Psychological analysis. *Political Psychology, 21*, 351–366.

10. The *kaffiyah* is the black and white checkered head scarf worn by many Palestinians. Although it is not exclusively Palestinian, it has become a symbol for the Palestinian struggle of national liberation and for solidarity with the Palestinian people.

As part of the effort to build a Seeds of Peace community, participants are all given the same green T-shirts to wear over the three weeks that they are at camp and are instructed to put away items with national symbols on them so as not to offend other members of the community.

11. The dialogue groups at Seeds of Peace consist of around twelve to fifteen young people (fourteen and fifteen years of age) from opposing sides of the various conflicts. The groups are balanced where nationalism and gender are concerned and stay together as a group for the duration of the three-week program.

12. Facilitators selected to work at Seeds of Peace come from a variety of backgrounds and use modalities to promote dialogue that range from drama and movement to oral history and visual arts. All have extensive experience working with groups in conflict.

MARIEKE VAN WOERKOM *is the director of education at Seeds of Peace, an international nonprofit organization dedicated to preparing teenagers from areas of conflict to promote peace.*

An innovative program being implemented in U.S. school systems teaches youth to integrate the skills of conflict management beyond academics to their social and civic lives.

3

Normalizing effective conflict management through academic curriculum integration: The example of Workable Peace

Stacie Nicole Smith, David Fairman

> I've learned that conflict is not what causes the problems in the world; it's the way that people deal with these conflicts that causes the problems.
> —Ninth-grade Workable Peace student

THREE WEEKS AFTER September 11, 2001, students in Allison Gearhy's tenth-grade World History I class in Newton, Massachusetts, put aside their planned lessons on ancient China to hold a dialogue about appropriate U.S. responses to terrorism. The U.S. response was an issue that touched them all, and emotions ran high. To guide the class in effective listening and communication skills,

This chapter was adapted from a chapter in the forthcoming book: Noddings, N. (ed.), *Educating Global Citizens: Challenges and Opportunities.* New York: Teachers College Press, © 2004 by Teachers College, Columbia University. All rights reserved.

NEW DIRECTIONS FOR YOUTH DEVELOPMENT, NO. 102, SUMMER 2004 © WILEY PERIODICALS, INC.

they used a framework for understanding and dealing with conflict created by Workable Peace, a curriculum project of the Consensus Building Institute.

The students were given four perspectives on possible U.S. responses to September 11, each represented by two recently published opinion pieces from newspapers or journals, and asked to choose the perspective that most resembled their own. They were then asked, in four groups, to map out their underlying perspectives on the conflict in order to better understand what was most important to them in this dialogue by focusing on their interests, beliefs, emotions, and identities. Finally, the students came together to express their needs, concerns, and beliefs and to compare and contrast their own perspective with that of their classmates.

In the discussion, students not only defended their own deeply felt views but were also asked to listen to, restate, and acknowledge the needs and concerns underlying their classmates' perspectives. Rather than scoring points or reaching agreements, the goal of this discussion was to develop a better understanding of how and why Americans might legitimately disagree on what the United States should do in response to the terrorist attacks. Among the skills that the students practiced were explaining their views clearly, listening actively, acknowledging others' legitimate concerns, brainstorming options that reflected the needs of all points of view, and examining how the key issues might be resolved in ways that would meet the primary needs and concerns of others. Thus, the students were introduced to a model of conflict resolution that they could use to process not only the crisis of September 11, but one that they could draw on when examining conflicts throughout the school year and for handling conflicts in their own lives.

School curriculum benefits of conflict resolution education

Conflict resolution education (CRE) grew out of several parallel efforts: integrating social justice into schools, concerns about safety and youth violence, and desires to enhance responsible citizenship.[1]

Today, CRE encompasses, or is a component of, a broad range of initiatives in schools: violence prevention programs, diversity and tolerance programs, law-related education, citizenship or civic education, peer mediation programs, and whole school change efforts.

Crawford and Bodine have discussed the developmental continuum of conflict resolution education.[2] To have a deep and lasting impact, effective conflict resolution education should begin in elementary school and continue through secondary school, focusing at each grade level on developmentally appropriate skills and behaviors. Elementary and middle schools provide settings for learning many foundational CRE concepts and behaviors. High school is particularly appropriate for the higher-level integration of knowledge and skills that students need to understand intergroup conflict in history and society and to draw lessons that apply to their lives and current events. Cognitively, teenagers can explore and analyze complex social issues. Developmentally, they are seeking and being cast into adult social roles and learning how their membership in ethnic, economic, and cultural groups will shape those roles. Academically and socially, adolescents are studying and experiencing conflict and find themselves confronting decisions about their own responses. And emotionally, they struggle with the complexity of integrating their feelings, wants, and values to make good decisions. High schools can appropriately and effectively teach young people to understand and respond to conflicts more effectively in their personal, social, and civic lives.

Despite this enormous educational opportunity, many high schools lack the mandate and the tools to teach such skills. This is true even in academic disciplines where issues of intergroup conflict are most directly addressed: history and social studies. According to the National Council for the Social Studies, "Learning the content and thinking skills necessary for students to make public policy decisions, operate successfully in a society to build consensus, and learn to negotiate and manage differences have been the bulkheads of the field."[3] Yet numerous studies of social studies curricula and lessons show minimal effort to promote dialogue or negotiation skills on controversial topics.[4] Most high school social studies classes do not teach students to analyze multiple sources of conflict or to see conflict from multiple perspectives. Most core classroom textbooks do not assess critically the strategies that leaders and groups have used to deal with conflict, or ask students to examine alternative responses and evaluate their potential costs and benefits. And rarely do students put themselves into the shoes of primary actors in historical conflicts, to try out for themselves different ways to meet their needs and uphold their values.

As an example of the treatment of complex intergroup conflict in history classes, one high school global studies textbook offers this description of the colonization of the Americas:

The capture of Montezuma resulted in the Aztec ruler giving Cortes huge quantities of gold objects in hope of gaining his freedom. Montezuma was eventually killed, and his golden treasure was melted down into bullion bars. Within three years, warfare and disease destroyed the Aztec trading and tributary empire. Cortes, in the name of the Spanish monarchy, became the new ruler of Mexico.[5]

As in this example, the conflicts presented in history and current events—between peoples, states, and social groups—are traditionally presented as facts and events, with little effort to examine the complex, underlying dynamics. Without an opportunity for structured and critical learning about intergroup conflict, students often draw their understanding from history's victors. The lessons they often learn include these: group identities are fixed, conflict is usually zero sum, and violence and coercion are not only common but often effective ways—maybe the only ways—to deal with intergroup conflict.

Stand-alone programs

For thirty years, concerned educators have been developing ways to teach conflict management skills to students in public schools. One common approach is teaching conflict resolution as an extracurricular activity (for example, in a peer mediation program) or an elective course (such as negotiation skills training), using content and examples from interactions with teachers, friends, and family. Such strategies can be called stand-alone or process curriculum because they are not designed to teach specific academic content in conjunction with conflict management skills.

Stand-alone programs have been found to offer significant benefits, especially in the elementary and middle school grades.[6] However, the stand-alone approach has several limitations. First, any program that is separate and distinct from the core academic focus of schools is vulnerable to short-term shifts in faculty and student interest. The vulnerability of such programs only grows as the spread of high-stakes standardized testing increases pressures to cover content. This is especially true in urban and lower-income schools, where testing pressures are often coupled with budget constraints on electives and other curricular "extras," squeezing out courses and activities focused on teaching social and civic skills.[7]

Second, even when such stand-alone programs remain, they run the risk of appearing "extra" to the students. If such courses or units are not given equal value in relation to academics by the school culture, students may be less likely to take them seriously. Students learn that what matters is the material on the tests required for graduation. Thus, if mediation and conflict resolution programs are devoid of academic content and disconnected from the knowledge of their core courses, they become a lower priority in the minds of students.

Connected to this is a third, and possibly the most important, limitation of nonintegrated approaches to civic and social skills: the relationship of these lessons to reality. The lessons about conflict within the academic curriculum are often lessons normalizing violence and coercion. If we want to affect the way young people think about and deal with conflict, we need to do so within the context of the conflicts they learn about in school. Conflict management skills taught in isolation are unlikely to overcome the assumptions and beliefs about conflict embedded in traditional social studies and history curricula. For all of these reasons, conflict resolution education is most effective when it is integrated into the academic curriculum.

A curriculum integration model: Workable Peace

There are a few alternatives to stand-alone approaches to teaching conflict resolution that schools, teachers, and students are likely to embrace and sustain. Although not many social studies and history curricula explicitly address intergroup conflict on a general sociological level, a few curriculum enrichment programs have succeeded on a broad scale in integrating new ways to teach about intergroup conflict and conflict resolution; an example is Facing History and Ourselves.

The Workable Peace curriculum aims to teach general concepts and skills of conflict analysis and management in the context of historical and current events selected for relevance to high school social studies and history curricula. The Workable Peace curriculum is a model for discussing what students can learn about conflict, how they can learn it, and the difference this can make.

Workable Peace is based at the Consensus Building Institute (CBI) in Cambridge, Massachusetts, a nonprofit organization dedicated to improving the theory and practice of public dispute resolution. The project was created and piloted in 1997 by an advisory board and staff of dispute resolution professionals—psychologists, political scientists, urban planners, philosophers—working with high school educators. Their goal was to translate state-of-the-art knowledge about the nature of conflict and conflict management into clear, practical, and evocative materials and pedagogy for high school social studies and history classes.

The Workable Peace curriculum has three main components: a conceptual framework, historical role plays, and civic learning projects that relate directly to students' lives.

The conceptual framework

At the heart of the curriculum is the Workable Peace Framework, a one-page summary of conflict management concepts and skills that the curriculum aims to teach (Figure 3.1). The Workable Peace Framework is an attempt to synthesize and distill forty years of knowledge from research and practice in intergroup conflict management. It incorporates academic and practitioner insights

Figure 3.1. The Workable Peace Framework

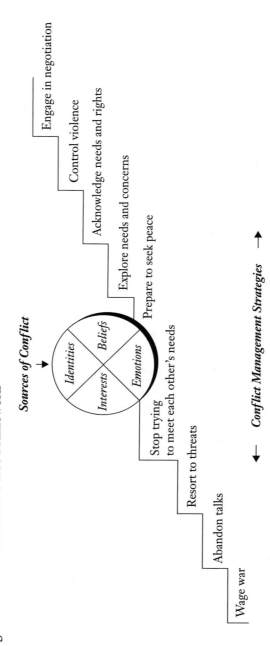

Sources of Conflict

Identities / Beliefs / Interests / Emotions

Wage war
Abandon talks
Resort to threats
Stop trying to meet each other's needs
Prepare to seek peace
Explore needs and concerns
Acknowledge needs and rights
Control violence
Engage in negotiation

← *Conflict Management Strategies* →

from fields of political science, social psychology, and multiparty negotiation into a one-page presentation of skills and behaviors.[8] The framework is designed to make conflict analysis accessible to teenagers and to provide a theoretical foundation for the more active, content-centered pieces of the curriculum. The curriculum contains a variety of activities to introduce the framework to students, including lessons on identifying and disentangling the sources of conflict, and to build their skills in particular areas, such as exploring the needs and concerns of others, managing strong emotions, and negotiating effectively.

Role plays

The core tool for teaching the framework is a series of role play units set in historical and current hot spots of intergroup conflict. Each unit centers on a major historical conflict that has been aligned with state and national curriculum standards for social studies and challenges students to resolve the issues at stake in the conflict. The role plays address conflict in ancient Greece, in American nineteenth-century labor history and the mid-twentieth-century civil rights movement, and in the contemporary Middle East, Guatemala, Northern Ireland, and Rwanda.

A role play is a type of learning by doing that allows participants an opportunity to develop direct experience with the content and skills being taught. Students take on the personality and background of an individual or group and interact with others in the context of a specific situation. Role play provides an opportunity for learners to internalize concepts, principles, and ideas through lived experience and reflection, leading to changes in behaviors and actions.[9] There are several educational theories about how this occurs, but all of them involve "a process of confronting our existing ideas about how and why certain things happen, breaking them down, and offering a new model or set of postulates to replace the old ones."[10]

It is one thing to know how to manage conflict but quite another to act on this knowledge, particularly in difficult situations where one's own needs are at stake, one's core beliefs are challenged, and one's emotions are intense. Practicing conflict management behaviors within a realistic role helps students to confront the psychological and interpersonal responses that are most difficult to manage in situations of real conflict. At the same time, role play provides a safe setting that allows students to experiment, reflect, and give and receive feedback.

At the end of role plays, teachers lead students through a debriefing. Students reflect on how well they met their own group's interests and upheld their values and identities, how well they did at reaching an agreement meeting the interests of all parties, how well they worked as a negotiating group, and what they would do differently next time. The debriefing also provides an opportunity to delve more deeply into the history, examine differences between the simulation outcomes and the actual outcomes, and look at the consequences of the actual outcome on the parties involved. A skillful teacher can generate an enormous amount of learning about conflict and conflict resolution through the debriefing, drawing on examples of specific moments in the negotiation process.

Civic learning

Civic learning, an important goal of most conflict resolution education, refers to the development of behaviors and practices connected to active democratic participation. Introducing new conceptual skills and trying them out in a simulated context lays the groundwork for the development of new behaviors and habits in response to conflict. However, the link needs to be made between the classroom context and the real conflicts in students' lives in order for students to apply the conflict management skills they learned. This approach is consistent with research on effective civic education, which shows that making explicit connections between historical and current situations is more likely to lead to real changes in student behavior.[11] By connecting back to real conflicts that students face, they explore the potential personal value of the skills and simulate the potential differences in outcomes they could expect by using these new skills in dealing with their own conflicts.

The third part of the Workable Peace curriculum, civic learning, encourages teachers to connect themes, skills, and lessons from the historical cases to conflicts occurring in the world today and in students' lives. Unlike stand-alone conflict management programs, Workable Peace uses conflict examples that may have personal relevance and evoke intense emotion—not as the skill teaching tools, but rather only after the major skills have been introduced, practiced, and reflected on. In this way, students develop skills in situations where using these skills does not threaten their personal identities since they are playing a role rather than being themselves. Now, civic learning asks them to apply those skills to situations where they may have more personally at stake, but only after they have had ample opportunity to experience the benefits of using these skills in solving problems and reaching acceptable agreements to conflicts.

What students learn

Workable Peace is designed to provide students with opportunities to learn a broad set of social, emotional, and civic skills for dealing with conflict, while learning current and historical facts and themes.

Disentangling the sources of conflict

When in a situation of conflict, one rarely stops to think about the multiple needs, concerns, and feelings that underlie the particular problem at hand. Often the parties involved do not share an understanding of what the problem is, what is at stake, or what options there are for resolution. In fact, individuals may not even clearly recognize what it is they hope to achieve, how their beliefs interact with the situation, or how their emotions are affecting their perceptions. This is especially true in conflicts faced by adolescents, who have less training and experience in difficult situations and less self-knowledge about the components of their perceptions. Such lack of clarity makes it difficult to engage in any constructive process of conflict management.

Workable Peace teaches students to understand the multiple causes of a conflict by taking conflicts apart and analyzing them piece by piece. Based on a synthesis of the literature on conflict factors, the Workable Peace Framework names four core sources of conflict: interests (what we and they want), beliefs (our views and theirs about what should be—values—and what is—perceptions of reality), identities (who we and they are, especially as members of social groups), and emotions (what we and they feel). Students are taught to name and disentangle these key components of conflict and use them to better understand the perceptions of opposing groups involved in conflict.[12]

An example

In a lesson about the 1962 Cuban missile crisis, students were divided into two groups and provided with letters and speeches from either Soviet Premier Nikita Khrushchev or U.S. President John F. Kennedy. The students used the documents to map out the sources of conflict—the interests, beliefs, emotions, and identities—from their perspective and from their ideas of the other perspective; they put this information in a table. The two groups of students then reconvened to share their work, and the teacher put the two finished tables side by side to form a four-column map of the conflict (Table 3.1).

Students can draw many lessons from such an exercise. First, before even looking at the table from the other perspective, students can analyze the different components of their perspective on the conflict. Knowing what is driving an actor in a conflict helps them understand the reasons underlying what they want. Khrushchev wanted to keep the missiles in Cuba, with one underlying interest of preventing a U.S. attack on Cuba. In addition, clarifying interests and focusing on them creates many more possibilities for resolving conflicts.[13] Khrushchev was ultimately able to meet his interest in preventing a U.S. attack on Cuba by gaining a noninvasion pledge from Kennedy in exchange for withdrawing the missiles.

Analysis of one's own sources of conflict may also elucidate interests, such as avoiding war, that conflict with other interests, beliefs,

Table 3.1. Differing perspectives on the Cuban missile crisis

	Perspective of Khrushchev		Perspective of Kennedy	
	Us	*Them*	*Us*	*Them*
Interests: "We want ___ because . . ."	• to defend Cuba's sovereignty • to help Cuba defend herself from U.S. attack • to support our international allies	• intimidation of USSR • to attack Cuba • no Russian influence in Cuba • removal of missiles	• removal of missiles from attack by USSR from Cuba • weapons removed from Cuba • no wish for war	• world domination • control of Cuba • ability to attack the U.S.
Beliefs: "We believe . . ."	• USSR's relationship with Cuba is not of U.S. concern • U.S. actions violate International Law; ours do not • missiles in Cuba are defensive	• the U.S. can issue ultimatums and threats with impunity	• U.S. peace is endangered by these missiles • USSR is violating promises • U.S. protects the democratic and capitalist countries of the world	• USSR can deceive the U.S. • provocation will go unchallenged
Emotions: "We feel . . ."	• indignant • pushed • justified	• powerful • superior	• confident • strong • justified	• righteous
Identities: "We are . . ."	• reasonable • supporters of Cuban freedom	• aggressors • imperialists • immoral	• peaceful • honest • patient • powerful • reasonable	• deceptive • aggressors

or identities, such as forcing a new governmental system in Cuba. This analysis helps students to see the trade-offs that are made in any decision and encourages them to weigh and prioritize their needs. For President Kennedy, the agreement with Khrushchev addressed the overriding U.S. interest in reducing the threat of a missile strike by the USSR. At the same time, it required trading off the U.S. interest in overthrowing Castro.

Disentangling a conflict may also highlight the role emotions play in driving or escalating conflict in ways that may work against interests or values. During the Cuban missile crisis, both U.S. and Soviet decision makers felt intense fear and anger that several times threatened to derail the negotiation process and escalate the conflict. As students identify and discuss emotions that the decision makers felt, they begin to appreciate not only the importance of emotions in historical conflicts, but also how they handle their own emotions in conflicts.

By using this model of conflict analysis, students develop a skill they can use on their own to deal with conflicts they experience around them and in their own lives. It provides a cognitive strategy for them to take time to think about what their needs, values, and emotions are before jumping to follow their impulses. And the more opportunity they have to practice this strategy in their course work, the more normalized it becomes and the more available it will be as a habit to draw on when conflicts strike in their own lives.[14]

Perspective taking

Members of groups in conflict—especially long-standing and violent conflict—have a tendency to delegitimize, stereotype, and ultimately dehumanize their opponents. Negotiation based on partial and biased perception of other groups' interests and needs and in an atmosphere of deep animosity is unlikely to be productive.[15] Conversely, dialogue focused on understanding the other can begin to break down stereotypes; highlight shared interests, values, and identities; and lay the basis for productive negotiation.[16]

Students using the Workable Peace curriculum begin developing perspective-taking skills during the conflict mapping activity described above by examining differences in how each group perceives itself and is perceived by others. Students can then consider the ways that perceptions and misperceptions can make it more difficult to deal productively with conflict. Similarly, they may see how it feels to face delegitimization by others and take measure of its costs. This exercise allows them to develop an appreciation of the value of dialogue in clarifying each other's perspectives and the costs of dismissing the other's needs and emotions as nonexistent, irrational, or irrelevant.

This point is made most clear during the role plays when participants have the opportunity to understand the differing perspectives of their negotiating partners and attempt to see how doing so can help them meet their own interests. In the role plays, students learn that it is impossible to develop solutions if they cannot agree on what the conflict is about, or if they do not know what needs the other side is trying to achieve. Therefore, participants are encouraged to engage in a process of exploration, with the goal of understanding how each group sees the situation and what each group hopes to achieve in a resolution.

By experiencing the effects of perspective taking during a conflict analysis or role-play exercise, students begin to understand how and why it can be helpful to them to learn about their conflicts from their adversary's point of view. In a study of our work with Israeli and Palestinian schools, Haifa University researchers found that after participating in Workable Peace role plays on other historical conflicts, students demonstrated substantial changes in their ability to see the Israeli-Palestinian conflict through the eyes of the other. To measure this, students were asked to write about the Israeli-Palestinian conflict from the point of view of the other side. In the pretest and control groups, students could write little or nothing from the viewpoint of the other. At posttest, virtually all of the Workable Peace students were able to write with understanding and empathy from the other group's perspective.[17]

Students in the United States have had similar responses about the value of this skill. One student reflected, "I feel I learned a significant amount about the importance of thinking about a situation through the perspective of another person. We must take time to think about what the people around us might be feeling about different situations. It is important not to assume that we know how they feel, but to try to explore their point of view in order to try to solve problems."

Acknowledgment, listening, and communication skills

Understanding is necessary but not sufficient for conflict resolution and improving relationships. Workable Peace also teaches the importance of acknowledging needs and rights (for example, the right to exist or to self-determination; the need for a living wage or a minimum level of profitability). Acknowledgment has two functions: psychologically, mutual acknowledgment can have a powerful transformative effect by overturning deeply held assumptions about the intentions and beliefs of opposing groups; strategically, acknowledgment of specific needs and rights creates a framework for negotiation by setting out issues to be addressed.[18]

During the role-play negotiations, there is often a turning point where a student voices the legitimacy of the needs, emotions, or experiences of a negotiating partner. Acknowledgment can dramatically increase willingness to work cooperatively or make trade-offs to resolve conflict. One student commented, "It was interesting in the Northern Ireland role play how the residents acknowledged the pains of the Orange Order and how they were getting hurt in the struggle. This changed the attitude of the Orange Order. With this new attitude the Orange Order seemed to try and give things up for the Catholics more readily."

With the help of a skilled teacher, the role plays also teach other critical communication skills that have been identified for effective social interaction: active listening and asking questions, modifying tone of voice and body language, dealing effectively with emotions, and reframing negative statements into positive statements.[19]

Negotiation skills

Although poor communication dramatically increases the probability that conflicts will continue or escalate, good communication on its own does not necessarily lead to resolution.[20] Effective negotiation skills, such as assessing interests and alternatives, inventing options, making trade-offs, and seeking objective criteria for decision making, can help parties translate understanding into concrete options and strategies for resolving issues that divide them.

Workable Peace teaches a mutual gains approach to negotiation developed at the Harvard-MIT-Tufts Program on Negotiation.[21] Students learn and practice this approach during the role plays, where they attempt to find resolutions that are better than the alternative: continued violent conflict. In addition to effective preparation and focusing on interests, key negotiation skills include inventing options and making wise trade-offs to reach agreement.

As noted above, students need to move beyond mutual understanding to generate options that could be better for all parties than their alternatives outside negotiation. Workable Peace teaches students to use a "what-if" approach. Rather than simply trading offers or criticizing each other's proposals, students should be asking each other why they want what they want and framing their proposals conditionally: "What if we tried a different option that could work for me and—if I'm understanding your interests—could work for you?" This approach makes the process of inventing options collaborative rather than adversarial. Imagining multiple alternatives fosters creativity because students are not yet seeking agreement, but rather brainstorming to look for possibilities worthy of further development.

Consider this example of students negotiating security arrangements in Hebron during the Middle East role play. The group was discussing two issues: control over the land in Hebron and maintaining security for Israeli settlers living in the core areas of the city. Israeli and Palestinian governmental representatives, Israeli military, and Palestinian police all agreed that after a period of five years without violence, all control over land in Hebron would be given to the Palestinians. In addition, the Israeli military would withdraw completely from Hebron, leaving the settlers under Palestinian protection. The Israeli settlers were highly opposed to this agreement:

SETTLER: If you get control of H2 area, why can't we keep the Israeli military to protect the settlers?

PALESTINIAN POLICE: We can't guarantee protection of Israelis within Hebron unless the military leaves. It's our city, and we aren't going to let you have Israeli control.

SETTLER: But we don't trust you. You have to understand, the Palestinian police is made up of former terrorists.

PALESTINIAN GOVERNMENT: Well, you're just going to have to trust us.

ISRAELI MILITARY: What if, during the five-year transitional period, you were able to develop trust in the Palestinian police, while the Israeli military remained in H2 and patrolled jointly with the Palestinian police?

In this example, the student playing the Israeli military role seeks to break a potential impasse and deal with mutual deep-seated distrust by proposing a transitional period as a "what-if."

Negotiators may be very effective at creating options, yet still face great difficulty reaching a final agreement; they need to find some objective principles, standards, or criteria, acceptable to all negotiators, to help them choose among the options. "Objective" here does not necessarily mean "right," but rather a reasonable way to make a decision and a rationale that can be used to sell the agreement to each negotiator's constituents. Examples include precedents from past negotiations, norms or rules that have been used to resolve similar issues, or the use of a mutually acceptable third party.

By integrating these negotiation skills through historically accurate role plays, Workable Peace not only helps students gain a deeper understanding of a particular conflict, but also helps foster a range of civic and social aptitudes, including creative thinking, problem solving, and moral reasoning. The benefits for students of integrating conflict resolution skills into their study of history include making decisions with others, discussing differences, solving problems, and dealing with emotions—in short, skills needed to participate effectively as democratic citizens. As one student wrote, "The role play does aid in strengthening conflict-resolving characteristics in a person. We learn how to look at the conflict through the other person's eyes, what things are and aren't beneficial to say or do in the process, and we learn how to settle the conflict so that both sides are happy."

Civic engagement and skills

One of the goals of the Workable Peace curriculum is to help students apply the concepts and skills learned through the Workable Peace Framework and role plays to intergroup issues and conflicts in their schools and communities. Using the historical and current curricular exercises to teach and practice these skills, Workable Peace works to normalize the effective use of conflict management to deal with conflicts. In addition, the curriculum provides a number of tools and activities for making the link back from the academic content to issues closer to students' lives. For example, the Northern Ireland role play on the annual marching season, which often heightens tensions or leads to violence between Catholics and Protestants, has a civic learning activity that draws on the theme of separating "turf," and asks students to examine turf and cliques in their own school and neighborhood. The Rwanda role play concludes with an activity that asks students to consider stereotypes of groups within their community and the impacts of relying and acting on these stereotypes in conflicts.

Teachers teaching and practicing conflict management

To get the most out of the curriculum, teachers must know not only how to logistically structure and manage the activities, but also how to watch for the teachable moments that arise during role plays and guide students' discussions about what they can learn from their experiences. This can be a serious challenge. As conflict resolution educator Ellen Raider observes, "Most adults in schools have had little preparation, training, or encouragement to manage their own conflicts cooperatively, let alone teach these skills to others."[22] To do this successfully, teachers not only need to understand the skills, they need opportunities to practice them. For this reason, comprehensive teacher training is important as preparation for implementing the Workable Peace curriculum. The standard three-day institute has the dual purpose of introducing teachers to the skills of conflict management and preparing them to integrate the curriculum into their classrooms. At the workshops, teachers are challenged to integrate these new concepts and skills into their own understandings and behaviors, as they simultaneously work to absorb the knowledge and pedagogy.

A more efficient and effective strategy for providing large numbers of teachers with the skills to institutionalize the teaching of conflict management would be to incorporate such preparation into preservice teacher education programs. Ideally, this would be integrated by using curriculum materials like Workable Peace in social studies methods courses. Teachers might also be offered role plays set around typical conflicts they will experience in classrooms and meeting rooms.

These strategies may go part of the way in helping to make integrated conflict management education possible in academic classrooms. However, left unspoken is the greatest challenge to teaching conflict management skills to teenagers: the believability factor. If students do not see their newly learned strategies reflected by the adults they interact with in their schools, communities, and world, the students' own implementation becomes more difficult. Without mentors and models, students may encounter difficulty in using these skills and tools.[23]

Conclusion

Where do young people learn about how to deal with conflict? They see and hear of these conflicts every day—in newspapers and on television, on the street and in their neighborhoods, and in their classrooms. Too often, popular and peer culture teach young people simplistic attitudes and aggressive behaviors that intensify these conflicts. Adolescents, who are forming their own identities, are too frequently encouraged by the media and their peers to exaggerate intergroup differences. And much of their academic curriculum on conflict focuses on the strategies of violence, while doing little to illustrate the complexity of these conflicts or provide a sense of alternative strategies.

By integrating conflict resolution into the academic curriculum, particularly in the social studies, where the study of conflict comprises much of the content, teachers provide an opportunity to deepen the lessons that students learn about intergroup conflict. By inviting students to disentangle and analyze conflict, examine history and current events from multiple perspectives, and take on the conflicts of history to attempt their own resolutions, teachers develop students' abilities to understand the underlying sources of conflict, engage constructively with those with whom they are in conflict, and practice skills for resolving conflicts without violence. By teaching and modeling these skills, we teach young people to make connections between conflicts around the world, in their home country, and in their own schools and communities.

Notes

1. Girard, K., & Koch, S. J. (1996). *Conflict resolution in the schools: A manual for educators.* San Francisco: Jossey-Bass.

2. Crawford, D., & Bodine, R. (1996). *Conflict resolution education: A guide to implementing programs in schools, youth-serving organizations, and community and juvenile justice settings.* Washington, DC: Office of Juvenile Justice and Delinquency Prevention, U.S. Department of Justice, and Office of Elementary and Secondary Education, U.S. Department of Education.

3. National Council on the Social Studies. (1994). *Expectations of excellence: Curriculum standards for social studies.* Washington, DC: Author. P. 3. See also Soley, M. (1996, Jan.). If it's controversial, why teach it? *Social Education*, 9–14.

4. Goodlad, J. (1983). *A place called school: Prospects for the future.* New York: McGraw-Hill. McNeil, L. (1986). *Contradictions of control.* New York: Routledge.

5. Willner, M., Hero, G., & Weiner, J. (1995). *Global studies.* New York: Barron's Educational Series. Vol. 2, p. 188.

6. Nakkula, M., & Nikitopoulos, C. (1996). *Preliminary evaluation findings for the fall 1995 implementation of the Program for Young Negotiators.* Cambridge, MA: Harvard University Graduate School of Education. Powell, K., Muir-McClain, L., & Halasyamani, L. (1995). A review of selected school-based conflict resolution and peer mediation projects. *Journal of School Health, 65,* 426–431.

7. Neill, M., & Gayler, K. (2001). Do high-stakes graduation tests improve learning outcomes? Using state-level NAEP data to evaluate the effects of mandatory graduation tests. In G. Orfield & M. L. Kornhaber (Eds.), *Raising standards or raising barriers? Inequality and high-stakes testing in public education.* New York: Century Foundation Press. Pp. 107–125.

8. Theoretical and practical work includes: Fisher, R., & Ury, W. (1983). *Getting to yes.* New York: Penguin Books. Fisher, R. (1993). The potential for peacebuilding: Forging a bridge from peacekeeping to peacemaking. *Peace and Change, 18,* 247–266. Horowitz, D. (1985). *Ethnic groups in conflict.* Berkeley: University of California Press. Jervis, R. (1978). Cooperation under the security dilemma. *World Politics, 30,* 167–213. Kelman, H. (1997). Social-psychological dimensions of international conflict. In I. W. Zartman & J. L. Rasmussen (Eds.), *Peacemaking in international conflict: Methods and techniques* (pp. 191–237). Washington, DC: U.S. Institute of Peace Press. Lake, D., & Rothchild, D. (1998). Spreading fear: The genesis of transnational ethnic conflict. In D. Lake & D. Rothchild (Eds.), *The international spread of ethnic conflict.* Princeton, NJ: Princeton University Press. Lax, D., & Sebenius, J. (1993). The power of alternatives or the limits to negotiation. In J. W. Breslin & J. Rubin (Eds.), *Negotiation theory and practice* (pp. 97–114). Cambridge, MA: Program on Negotiation Books. Rubin, J., Pruitt, D., & Kim, H. S. (1994). *Social conflict: Escalation, stalemate and settlement* (2nd ed.). New York: McGraw-Hill. Schelling, T. (1960). *The strategy of conflict.* Cambridge, MA: Harvard University Press. Tellis, A., Szayna, T., & Winnefeld, J. (1997). *Anticipating ethnic conflict.* Santa Monica, CA: RAND.

9. Dewey, J. (1938). *Experience and education.* New York: Macmillan.

10. Susskind, L., & Corburn, J. (2000). Using simulations to teach negotiation: Pedagogical theory and practice. In M. Wheeler (Ed.), *Teaching negotiation: Ideas and innovations* (pp. 285–310). Cambridge, MA: PON Books.

11. Carnegie Corporation. (2003). *The civic mission of schools.* New York: Carnegie Corporation of New York and the Center for Information and Research on Civic Learning and Engagement.

12. The Workable Peace Framework draws especially from Fisher, R. (2000). Intergroup conflict. In M. Deutsch & P. Coleman (Eds.), *The handbook of conflict resolution* (pp. 166–184). San Francisco: Jossey-Bass. Horowitz. (1985). Kelman (1997). Rubin et al. (1994). Tellis et al. (1997).

13. Fisher & Ury. (1981).

14. Raider, E. (1995). Conflict resolution training in schools: Translating theory into applied skills. In J. Rubin (Ed.), *Conflict, cooperation, and justice* (pp. 93–121). San Francisco: Jossey-Bass.

15. Rothman, J. (1997). *Resolving identity based conflict in nations, organizations and communities.* San Francisco: Jossey-Bass.

16. Fisher. (1997). Kelman. (1997). Rubin et al. (1994).

17. Lustig, I. (2001). *The effects of studying distant conflicts on the perception of a proximal one.* Unpublished master's thesis, University of Haifa.

18. Kelman. (1997).

19. Raider. (1995).

20. Krauss, R., & Morsella, E. (2000). Communication and conflict. In M. Deutsch & P. Coleman (Eds.), *The handbook of conflict resolution* (pp. 131–143). San Francisco: Jossey-Bass.

21. See especially Consensus Building Institute. (2000). *Teaching the mutual gains approach.* Cambridge, MA: Consensus Building Institute. Fisher & Ury. (1983). Sebenius, J. (1992). Negotiation analysis: A characterization and review. *Management Science, 38,* 18–39. Susskind et al. (1999).

22. Raider. (1995).

23. Feldman, S. S., & Elliott, G. R. (1990). *At the threshold: The developing adolescent.* Cambridge, MA: Harvard University Press. Feldman & Elliott. (1990).

STACIE NICOLE SMITH *is a senior associate at the Consensus Building Institute in Cambridge, Massachusetts, and the director of Workable Peace.*

DAVID FAIRMAN *is the managing director at the Consensus Building Institute and codirector of Workable Peace.*

A conflict management program developed to support the transition from a closed to open society in postcommunist eastern and central Europe focuses on the future leaders of this region: adolescents.

4

After the fall: A conflict management program to foster open society

Daniel L. Shapiro

THE FALL OF THE Berlin Wall rocked the sociopolitical equilibrium of eastern and central Europe. Communism lost its grip over much of Europe. The USSR, Yugoslavia, and Czechoslovakia divided along ethnic, religious, and historical lines. Ethnopolitical tensions surfaced across the region, and in Yugoslavia, tensions combusted. Whereas democracy was supposed to bring wealth, freedom, and hope to eastern and central Europe, the immediate consequences of postcommunism were violence, economic instability, and political unpredictability.

Beyond the urgent task of crisis management, an incredible amount of work was needed to support the transition from a closed to an open society. For over forty years, people in communist-bloc countries had learned from leaders like Stalin and Ceausescu that the best way to deal with differences was to suppress them through force and fear. But once communism had fallen, how could people deal with their differences in a way that could sustain an open society?

With funding from the Soros Foundation,[1] I developed a conflict management program that has reached nearly 1 million youth

NEW DIRECTIONS FOR YOUTH DEVELOPMENT, NO. 102, SUMMER 2004 © WILEY PERIODICALS, INC.

in twenty-one former communist-bloc countries: Albania, Bosnia-Herzegovina, Belarus, Bulgaria, Croatia, Czech Republic, Estonia, Hungary, Kazakhstan, Kyrgyzstan, Lithuania, Latvia, Moldova, Macedonia, Poland, Romania, Russia, Serbia and Montenegro, Slovenia, Slovakia, and Ukraine.[2] The program was designed to equip youth with skills to deal effectively with interpersonal and intergroup conflicts in an open society. Program development began in 1991. Implementation of the program's curriculum into eastern and central Europe began in 1995 and is ongoing.

This chapter examines some of the challenges in building the conflict management program, as well as some of its accomplishments in helping youth shift toward an open society.

The need: A lack of skills to deal with intergroup differences

With communism officially gone and the infrastructure of capitalism not yet built, the resulting economic, political, and social vacuum was ripe for conflict. The many differences between people of varied ethnic, religious, and national groups that had been suppressed under communism were now out in the open. People were free to deal with their differences, but after living in a closed society for forty-five years, they had few skills to do so.

These countries were in desperate need of immediate political, economic, and diplomatic assistance to build political infrastructure and to prevent the spread of conflict across regions. The United Nations came to assist. Nongovernmental organizations (NGOs) began to reemerge.

Yet little attention was placed on the future leaders of those regions: the adolescents. They would eventually inherit the heavy weight of sociopolitical responsibility. Long-term transitional effectiveness depended on their motivation and ability to ingest and live the ideas of freedom and democracy inherent in the concept of an open society.

For these reasons, adolescents became the target population of the conflict management program. The program targeted students ages ten to fourteen, although high school and university students also used the program's curriculum. Adolescents were young enough to be open to learning new ways to deal with their conflicts, and they were old enough to have the cognitive and emotional capacities necessary to manage conflicts constructively. Research suggests that individuals from approximately ages ten to adult have the ability to understand and appreciate the motivations and emotions of others without the intervention of a third party.[3]

The program also worked with teachers. They held much of the responsibility for helping the students learn the values and skills needed to operate successfully in their new society. The program focused on both teaching students and training teachers in the methodology used to spread conflict management skills to the youth. The conflict management program was formulated as a train-the-trainer program and was integrated into classrooms and after-school activities.

The framework of the conflict management program

In 1992, I began writing the conflict management program's core curriculum, *Conflict and Communication: A Guide Through the Labyrinth of Conflict Management.*[4] The activities in the curriculum were field-tested in classrooms in eighteen eastern and central European countries.

The curriculum became the basis of the conflict management program and was initiated into schools in eastern Europe beginning in 1995. The curriculum's goals were to enable students to learn to analyze their attitudes and perspectives critically, develop useful skills for managing conflicts, understand the importance of clear, two-way communication, and improve on their ability to communicate in ways that defuse conflict.[5]

Since 1995, the curriculum has been used in schools, NGOs, universities, religious groups, government organizations, youth clubs organized by local authorities, and many other institutions throughout the twenty-one countries. It has been integrated into thousands of schools and approved by the ministry of education in several countries.[6] Each country's local Soros affiliates or trainers developed and administered their own version of the program to fit the needs of their country.[7] The program has taken a different form in many of the countries, depending on the visions of the local Soros Foundation affiliates. In the Czech Republic, for example, the curriculum is taught in schools, whereas in Moldova, the curriculum activities are facilitated for people in towns and small villages.

NGOs other than the Soros Foundation have been involved in funding and implementation. For example, in Macedonia, an education program called Promotion of Human Values designed a manual based on information from the conflict management program's core curriculum and funded by the International Committee of the Red Cross. In Latvia, the conflict management program's curriculum has been used extensively by youth clubs and schools in both the Latvian and Russian communities, partially funded by the United Nations and the World Health Organization. In Lithuania, the Youth Career and Advising Center has used the activities in the youth criminal justice system. In Slovenia, the curriculum has been used in pedagogical institutes and universities. During the Bosnian war, Bosnian refugees living in Ljubljana, Slovenia, taught the curriculum to students in refugee camps. And in Debrecen, Hungary, refugees were taught lessons from the curriculum.

The need served by the curriculum

There were two major needs of the emerging democracies of eastern and central Europe. First, a sturdy sociopolitical and economic infrastructure was needed to replace the old communist system. A number of groups assisted with this task, including NGOs, academics, businesspeople, the United Nations, and governmental representatives. They advised eastern and central European leaders and trained citizens in how to start a private business.

It was the second need of these emerging democracies, the psychosocial transformation of the society, that I emphasized in the curriculum. Teachers and students needed to learn the skills and values necessary to deal effectively with one another within their new political, social, and economic infrastructure. Many teachers were victims of the old habit and found it hard to adapt to the new sociopolitical system. They had grown up with the ideology of communism. They belonged to the Pioneers, a youth group based on communist ideology. Their role models included Stalin, Ceausescu, Zhivkov, and other communist leaders who used power and authority as the basis for decision making. Consequently, despite the fall of communism, many teachers had maintained their ideological beliefs with little more than a titular change in ideological affiliation. Yet their interpersonal behaviors had not shifted toward those intrinsic to an open society. They did not know how to embrace civic participation. They knew authoritarian decision making and did not know how to engage in open dialogue of differences. Students did not have the skills because there were no role models, so they had to learn them, sometimes side by side with their teachers.

Conceptual framework of the curriculum

While the conceptual framework of the conflict management program is probably applicable in any society, its basic subject areas were designed to address the transitional challenges of youth in eastern and central Europe, specifically the psychological shift of the students. In a democracy such as the United States, most students are accustomed to the freedom to make choices about what music to listen to, which presidential candidate to support, and what radio or television program to watch; there is no single, supreme doctrine that they must follow. In contrast, in communist Europe, the old state mentality did not allow students to be different; they were expected to support the government and were not allowed to challenge its thinking. In most communist-bloc countries, television and radio were tightly controlled by the state, as were governance, food rations, and employment.

With this authoritarian backdrop, students learned that the conflict management curriculum was different from other curricula they had used. It provided information and skills that helped them to communicate, cooperate, and manage conflicts constructively. These were skills foreign to the closed culture in which they were raised. From the first lesson, they learned that there are specific skills they needed to know that would help them deal with their peers, families, and community. They learned that these skills of conflict management were organized into six major subject areas. The activities they experienced in each subject area helped them change their form of communication from the authoritarian style to an open communication.

The overview of each of the six subject areas that follows, along with an analysis of their relevance to eastern Europe, includes reflections from two Romanian school counselors, a Hungarian psychologist, and a Macedonian teacher and conflict management expert.[8]

"Me." During communism, people were not taught to know themselves as individuals. The collective interest was emphasized; the individual interest was neglected. Thus, the first subject area of the conflict management curriculum was called "Me." Activities in this area emphasized the importance of knowing oneself—of having adequate awareness of who one is and what one values. Students learned they can better manage conflicts when they have a sense of their own identity.

Ruxandra Tudose, a Romanian school counselor, notes that self-agency is in direct contrast to the state's mission of forming a monolithic sociopolitical culture:

After the fall of communism, the Romanian people were left with little sense of who we were as individuals. The essential characteristic of communism was treating people as a homogeneous group. Even if this equality was not real, what actually happened is that being treated as homogeneous for forty-five years, we started believing and feeling as we were treated. All students had to wear the same uniform. Starting at the age of four, children were involved in political organizations such as the Pioneers. Everyone had to participate in periodic political meetings, and everybody was required to join the Communist party as a member. Otherwise, a person's ascendance in career would be severely impaired.

Both children and adults were required to take part in grandiose festivals where everybody had to praise the regime, and especially the president, in poems, songs, painting, and dancing. For one month in the fall, schools and factories took part in community work, called "patriotic work," which actually meant agricultural harvesting of the land for the state. In addition to controlling the Romanian people's behavior, Ceausescu tried to control our thinking. He wanted the state to be in complete control of the people's mental activities.

"You." Students desperately needed skills to understand and deal with intergroup differences, another area that communism failed to address. The program's second subject area therefore focused on understanding the "other." Students learned that misperceptions and misunderstandings can easily arise in a conflict, harm relationships, and derail the conflict management process. To address this subject area, students participated in experiential activities to learn about the dangers of stereotyping, prejudice, and discrimination.

The activities helped students to gain an appreciation of the similarities and differences between themselves and others. This was a new concept for most of them. Under the old state mentality, people were all supposed to be the same. Of course, differences still existed; they were just ignored.

During the beginning years of this curriculum's implementation, tensions were rising in several countries. Bosnia-Herzegovina was already in a state of war, and nationalism was growing. As Romanian counselor Veronica Bogorin recalls,

Despite communism's emphasis on homogeneity, differences between individuals and groups did exist in Romania. They were just neglected, ignored, or suppressed. On the one hand, this kept animosities between groups from flaring. (Still, some groups were discriminated against, such as the gypsies.) On the other hand, there was little valuing of diversity under communism. Everybody was treated as a stereotyped automaton of the state. Everybody received the same amount of food rations at the market. Everybody received the same paycheck despite variations in work ability, motivation, and productivity.

"Me and You." Interpersonal communication was restrained during the years of communism. People feared that they might say something that would threaten the monolithic supremacy of the State. Therefore, after understanding "Me" and "You," students learned tools to communicate effectively between "Me and You." This area highlighted ways to foster a cooperative conversation in

which each person learned about his or her own interests and emotions and those of the other. Students learned skills to improve their awareness of body language, encourage information sharing, and enhance listening and trust.

In describing the restrictiveness of communication under communism, Hungarian psychologist Falus Gabor states:

At home we talk freely, yet in a quiet voice, because the walls are thin. There is code of trust that exists within the family. But this code of trust ends at our front door. Nothing is discussed outside our home. Once outside the door, we put on a different face. We learn to speak in circles. We don't make definite statements because they could incriminate us. And we learn never to trust anyone.[9]

Ruxandra Tudose from Romania notes:

Communism was a serious impediment to open communication. In Romania, access to information by the government was restrained. There were only two hours of television broadcasting daily, consisting mainly of Ceausescu's speeches and activities. Newspapers were comparable propaganda of the State. Access to literature was severely restricted. And correspondence from outside the country was censored. There was a strong need for intercultural communication; people were hungry for culture. The intellectuals managed to access literature through the black market, and everybody listened to the Free Europe radio station, which was broadcast from Germany. But everybody kept it as a big secret.

"Me vs. You." During communism, people did not openly express their differences. As stated by Darko Jordanov, a teacher and conflict management consultant from the Republic of Macedonia:

Part of the communist ideology was to pretend peace. Everybody must be equal and the same. . . . It is not realistic. I compare it to a race. My ideal is that everybody starts the race at the same time, but the one who runs the fastest is the winner. In communism, everybody was supposed to reach the end of the race at the same moment. . . . I see that it kills the race. . . . That is one of the reasons for the death of communism.[10]

Despite good communication skills and the best of intentions, the youth of eastern and central Europe naturally would experience conflicts with friends, family, and teachers. In the "Me vs. You" subject area, students directly examined the assumptions they held about conflict. While students commonly perceive conflicts as "bad" and "violent," they came to reconceptualize conflict as a disagreement between people that can be dealt with in cooperative or adversarial ways. They learned that nearly every conflict has positive potential and holds opportunity for growth and learning.[11]

Veronica Bogorin from Romania reflects on the connotations attached to the concept of conflict in Romania:

> The concept of "conflict" was understood as "conflict with the state." And no one wanted that. To disagree with the Communist party in public or in private was a serious crime. Everyone feared an invisible enemy who could hear through the walls or keyholes, who could be your neighbor, your best friend, or your brother-in-law. This fear made people unwilling to express their real opinions and feelings.

"Me with You." Many of the communist-bloc leaders ruled with an iron fist. Toughness, violence, and authoritarian decision making trumped collaboration. This adversarial process left many people's interests unmet, and people lacked role models to demonstrate the skills of collaborative negotiation.

Therefore, in the subject area of "Me with You," students learned a simple strategy to manage conflicts cooperatively. Based on ideas of interest-based negotiation,[12] the strategy consisted of five steps:

1. Recognize that a conflict exists.
2. Acknowledge feelings and what may have stimulated them.
3. Explore what each person wants from the conflict.
4. Brainstorm options for meeting each person's interests.
5. Decide on a plan that meets each person's interests.

This simple strategy was in direct opposition to the old system. When asked about similarities and differences between this strategy and those used commonly under communism, Ruxandra Tudose responded:

Big differences. In this new approach, conflicts must be recognized, something that did not occur under communism. Under communism, the government of course could not control people's feelings. But they did not allow them to speak about them especially if they did not favor the party lines. During the communist regime, students were told what and how to think, and brainstorming was in direct opposition to that mentality. Finally, deciding on a plan involves decision making. During the old regime, these skills were contradictory to the communist philosophy. The resolution of differences between people was based on hierarchical structure. Decisions were made by the person who had more authority. In a conflict between a teacher and student, for example, the opinion of the teacher would overrule any justification by the student. Similarly, the mandates of the communist leadership were to be followed without question. Negotiation was a sign of opposition to authority and ultimately to the hegemony of the State.

"Us." Whether or not students use the five-step strategy for dealing with their conflicts, why should they treat one another nonviolently and with adequate respect? Stalin, Ceausescu, and other communist leaders used violence to serve the interests of the state and themselves. What, if anything, should stand in the way of one student's simply using violence to force his or her way?

The final subject area of the curriculum, "Us," suggested that conflict management can be enacted in ways consistent with international principles of human rights. The behavior of disputants is subject to the limitations of accepted principles of human rights, such as those defined in the Declaration of Human Rights of Children.[13] By becoming aware of basic human rights, students could protect themselves from human rights violations and could stand up for their basic human rights.

The challenge ahead: Balancing freedom and responsibility

The conflict management program attempts to help eastern and central Europeans in the transition toward an open society. It teaches basic skills in how to understand oneself, others, and effective processes of conflict management.

Many of the people in eastern and central Europe are only beginning to realize the great responsibilities that come with freedom. According to Ruxandra Tudose,

What is the situation like now in 2004? Romanians acknowledge the fact that they can express their opinions freely on any topic, but they do so abusively, leading many to conclude that "the only right we earned is to mock others." Some people know their rights; others do not. And those who know their rights have few skills about how to assert those rights within a democratic framework where everyone is free up to the point that he or she impinges on the freedom of others. This program should be mandatory in all schools.

The transition from a closed to an open society is a long process. It continues to test the personal strength and courage of the individuals in eastern and central Europe. Their entire world has changed, and they are in the process of changing with it. To deal with differences more effectively will perhaps be their greatest challenge and their most meaningful success.

Notes

1. The Soros Foundation, established by financier and philanthropist George Soros, funds programs that promote the concept of an open society. According to the Soros Foundation Web site (http://www.soros.org/about/faq#a_whatisosi), "An open society is a society based on the recognition that nobody has a monopoly on the truth, that different people have different views and interests, and that there is a need for institutions to protect the rights of all people to allow them to live together in peace. Broadly speaking, an open society is characterized by a reliance on the rule of law, the existence of a democratically elected government, a diverse and vigorous civil society, and respect for minorities and minority opinions. The term 'open society' was popularized by the philosopher Karl Popper in his 1945 book *Open Society and Its Enemies*. Popper's work deeply influenced George Soros, the founder of the Open Society Institute, and it is upon the concept of an open society that Soros bases his philanthropic activity."

2. These are the current names of the countries included in the conflict management program. Note that "Serbia and Montenegro" is the official name of the federation of these two republics.

3. Selman, R. (1981). The development of interpersonal competence: The role of understanding in conduct. *Developmental Review, 1*, 401–422.

4. Shapiro, D. L. (1995). *Conflict and communication: A guide through the labyrinth of conflict management.* New York: Open Society Institute. I received helpful feedback from mentors and colleagues at Johns Hopkins University,

especially Jerome D. Frank. Professor Frank wrote the Foreword to the conflict management program's core curriculum. He suggests that war can be averted if we work simultaneously for verifiable, enforceable universal disarmament and substitution of effective nonviolent for violent methods of resolving conflicts.

5. Shapiro (1995).

6. The conflict management program contacted key trainers in eighteen countries to gather rough estimates of curriculum usage. In the Czech Republic, for example, the curriculum is being used in over ten thousand schools. In Latvia, the curriculum has been used by over fifty thousand students. The usage is comparably high in many of the countries.

7. The conflict management program has not yet been statistically evaluated. Evaluations to date have been qualitative, based on discussions, surveys, and questionnaires with trainers, administrators, and students involved in the program. The findings clearly support the utility of the program in helping students understand more about themselves and others, about how to deal with differences nonviolently, and about how to communicate effectively.

8. The reflections of Romanian school counselors Ruxandra Tudose and Veronique Bogorin are extracted from our e-mail communications in September 2003 and January 2004.

9. Shapiro, S., with Shapiro, R. (2004). *The curtain rises: Oral histories of the fall of communism in Eastern Europe.* Jefferson, NC: McFarland.

10. Coser, L. (1956). *The functions of social conflict.* New York: Free Press.

11. Shapiro, S., with Shapiro, R. (2004).

12. Fisher, R., Ury, W., & Patton, B. (1991). *Getting to yes: Negotiating agreement without giving in.* New York: Penguin.

13. See http://www.uncrc.info/. Parts of the Declaration on the Rights of the Child were reprinted in the conflict management program's curriculum (with permission of the United Nations).

DANIEL L. SHAPIRO *is an instructor in psychology in the Department of Psychiatry at Harvard Medical School/McLean Hospital and an associate at the Harvard Negotiation Project at Harvard Law School.*

Youth in war-ridden Burundi embrace the skills of conflict management in their process to become positive participants in their country's political process.

5

Youth Intervention for Peace Project: Burundi case study

Jean-Paul Bigirindavyi

THE EXPERIENCE OF Rwanda's genocide in 1994 shocked the world into disbelief as Western media finally focused their attention on the region's ongoing conflict. Yet little is being done today to prevent the reproduction of a parallel disaster in its twin country, Burundi, where similar conflict patterns may spark another intensely violent civil dispute. The death count has already reached an estimated 300,000 since 1993.[1] While efforts for peace focus on higher levels of diplomacy and negotiation, the situation of community interethnic violence in Burundi and, in particular, the fundamental role of youth in it, have largely been ignored.

Despite the encouraging developments of a peace process and cease-fire agreement, Burundi's civil society and community structure remains divided along the lines of its two major ethnic groups: Hutu and Tutsi. Without a social infrastructure to support peace and withstand violence at the community level, Burundi's chance for sustained peace is threatened. Conflict analyst Jan van Eck warns that Burundi is in a "terrible situation" with potentially devastating humanitarian consequences, particularly now, as the

NEW DIRECTIONS FOR YOUTH DEVELOPMENT, NO. 102, SUMMER 2004 © WILEY PERIODICALS, INC.

Burundian government faces a major, multifaceted transition.[2] Alison Des Forges of Human Rights Watch observes that Burundians see the current situation "as a time of fear, not a time of hope."[3] This is a chilling reminder of the Rwandan tragedy. There, all efforts were invested in the Arusha peace process, yet at the grassroots levels, intense fear and hatred escalated to the eruption of the 1994 genocide.

The violence in such conditions is vicious and systematic. In Burundi, the culture of violence and intimidation permeates society, so that even small disputes often end in violence. In order to transform this culture of violence, it is imperative to develop a comprehensive peace-building program that is capable of penetrating communities and reconstructing the relationships of the people who live within them.

This chapter presents an innovative intervention for conflict management being implemented in Burundi, the Youth Intervention for Peace Project.

Historical context

Burundi presents a striking example of the complexity of interethnic conflict. Although a person's specific ethnicity in Burundi can be ambiguous, ethnicity has retained a strong influence in political struggles. Burundi has three indigenous ethnic groups: the Hutu, who make up approximately 85 percent of the native population; the Tutsi, who make up approximately 14 percent; and the Twa, who make up just 1 percent. Conflicts over power have been divided along ethnic lines—between Hutu and Tutsi.

The historical derivation of each of these ethnic identities is complex. Because facts, lore, and misinformation have become intertwined, extracting an undisputed truth is impossible. From a sociological perspective, however, Burundi is actually a monoethnic country. All three ethnic groups—Hutu, Tutsi, and Twa—possess a common history for the past several hundred years, as well as shared language, traditions, and religion. Intermarriage between the groups has been common. Still, historical and social interpretations continue to separate these groups—not on a cultural or linguistic basis but on the grounds of physical features and social class.[4] The legacy of hatred and distrust between Hutu and Tutsi in Burundi is long. When Burundi broke away from Belgium's colonial rule in 1962, it inherited a society distorted by bitter ethnic division, a few educated elite torn by rivalry, and a system of patronage that has emphatically bred corruption. Burundi's autonomy came with no foundation of national unity.

The four decades of postindependent rule have been characterized by intimidation, political exclusion by the elite, economic segregation, and ethnic assertiveness. Structural violence and episodes of ethnic aggression have produced a volatile political, economic, and social situation that made the recent hostilities seem inevitable.

The turning point in the Burundian crisis came October 21, 1993, when the first democratically elected president, a Hutu, was assassinated by the Tutsi-dominated military, producing a chain of reactionary violent riots by the Hutu. With fresh memories of past massacres of Hutu in 1972 and 1988, the incident stirred emotional responses and led to preemptive attacks on the Tutsi population. Meanwhile, the military went on a rampage, killing key Hutu officials, as well as any other Hutu daring to protest. As the cycle of violence was set into motion, youth emerged as the vehicle of force.

The challenge of an ethnic conflict

As competition for domination escalates into violence, young people are exposed more to the divisive interpretations of their heritage than to inclusive versions. Thus, although there is no clear ethnic distinction between Hutu and Tutsi, the conflict that engulfs Burundi is seen and characterized, from both inside the country and the outside, as an ethnic struggle, where rival elites from the major ethnic groups viciously compete for domination of political and economic institutions. This rivalry, ignited decades ago, has caused the violence between the two ethnic groups to escalate to the current volatile situation. And young people have become the central tools in this political and ethnic violence.

The role of youth in interethnic violence has been recognized by the international community. In December 2002, Secretary-General Kofi Anan of the United Nations Security Council identified Burundi as one of five conflict-ridden countries where children were being used as soldiers.[5] The intensity of the recruitment by all sides—governmental troops, rebel forces, and militia groups—depicts how crucial a role the youth play in this intergroup conflict.

Ethnic violence has important, unique implications for youth. First, it manifests itself as either systematic or sporadic communal violence, where young people do most of the killing. Second, from the youths' perspective, it is a process driven not by politics but by their desire to achieve individual and collective security. Third, it is a process of expression by which youth achieve a sense of purpose, control, and power. Fourth, it is a process driven by promises of future opportunity:

- Ethnic violence as communal interaction. Ethnic violence turns communities into segregated neighborhoods that function as nuclei for indoctrinating youth in ethnic tension and sustaining a cycle of violent action.
- Ethnic violence as an effort to achieve security. As a community turns violent, security become essential, and violence seems to be a solution. When the community infrastructure breaks down, youth feel powerless to act or to participate in governance. In an effort to stop feeling victimized and to achieve a sense of power and security, they resort to violence. From a social-psychological perspective of conflict, youth are attracted to armed groups because the individual fear is intertwined with the collective fear of group.[6]
- Ethnic violence as an expression of purpose, control, and power. One important aspect of youth involvement in ethnic violence is the youth's perception of violence as a means to assert their place in the struggle. They may gain a sense of purpose as guardians of their ethnic group and experience feelings of importance, control, and power.

- Ethnic violence as a means to a better future. Ethnic violence is a process driven by the promise of a better future and a sense of social value for those actively involved. Youth expect to overcome their feelings of powerlessness and vulnerability when others involved in the conflict promise them recognition and liberation.

In the Burundian crisis, these four theoretical assertions play out in a complex way, making violence a seemingly legitimate way for young people to understand themselves and reassert their place in society. By participating in violence, young people gain an illusion of the power, self-esteem, and control they lack. Violence becomes an expression of revolt as well as resolution.

The Burundi crisis involves an overwhelming number of refugees and displaced people. Refugee and displacement camps prevent young people from establishing stability, making them feel homeless, invaluable, and degraded. Youth motivated to improve their situation may react violently. It is no surprise, then, that refugee and displacement camps are breeding grounds for ethnic indoctrination and recruitment for armed groups.

The situation in Burundi exemplifies the consequences of excluding youth from the conflict resolution process. While the peace process at the top levels of government remains critical for resolving the conflict, the fact that youth are not part of that process makes the attainment of peace or the cessation of violence unlikely. Excluded from the resolution process, young people respond with continuing violence.

A model for community conflict management programs

Effective management of interethnic violence begins with an understanding that youth violence, when it occurs, is an integral part of the intergroup conflict rather than secondary to it. It also requires a recognition that a key goal of conflict management should be to stop ignoring the fundamental values of the young people involved and instead provide outlets and channels for them to express these values in constructive ways. Young people need to be involved in the conflict resolution process, to have that process address their needs and concerns, and to learn new skills for nonviolent interaction.

Applying these fundamental themes, the Youth Intervention for Peace Project (YIPP) began as a way to address interethnic conflict in Burundi. Its principal focus is to restore youth relationships in order to foster a sense of security among this group and eradicate fear and distrust, and to transform the organized forces of violence into a grassroots nonviolent social movement where recognition is accorded, opportunity is available for all, and security is sustained.

The ultimate vision for YIPP is to transform youth violence into constructive nonviolent action. YIPP provides a way for youth to engage in community and national transformation and to understand and contextualize the violence in which they had participated and its implications for society. When youth become key players in society and nation building, they experience the satisfaction of constructive participation, control, and fulfillment.

In order to accomplish this mission, YIPP set five key programmatic goals:

- Establish permanent focal points (that is, affiliates of YIPP located across Burundi) with youth leaders in each district of Bujumbura, as well as outlying provinces.
- Through these focal points, conduct a series of intercommunity peace dialogues and peace-building training seminars.
- Create youth peace clubs to promote interactive activities and advance mutual empowerment.
- Offer community service projects to nurture a mutual dependency between rival ethnic groups and to foster cooperation.
- Establish a rehabilitation and integration program to assist youth returnees from refugee and displacement camps and ex-combatants.

Focal points

To create focal points with competent and proactive youth leaders in each geographical zone, YIPP leaders initiated interactive dialogues with key activist young people representing different ethnicities, both genders, and various socioeconomic groups. They introduced the concept of the role of youth in sustaining peace, as well as YIPP's thematic approach to youth violence. During these informal interactions, key volunteers were assigned to plan an initial workshop and begin recruiting participants. From the start, YIPP recognized that it was important to give control and ownership to the youth in setting up this project, using local resources, interactions, and understanding. This model is an extension of John Paul Lederach's elicitive mode of training.[7]

Participants for the workshop were selected carefully to ensure the inclusion of representatives from the diverse communities and backgrounds that make up Bujumbura's population. Again, ethnicity, gender, and socioeconomic backgrounds were among the criteria used to select participants. Age was also a consideration: participants were considered only if they were thirty-five years or younger. The goal was to have sixty individuals at the workshop representing all different zones in Bujumbura.

The initial workshop consisted of two areas of emphasis: interactive dialogues and peace training seminars. The intercommunity peace dialogues underscored the need for unity among young people. The peace training seminars that followed provided practical skill development in the areas of conflict resolution, nonviolent action, consensus building, and leadership. Sessions concluded with an opportunity for evaluation by participants.

Intercommunity peace dialogues

The objective of the intercommunity peace dialogues was to engage young people from rival ethnic groups in interaction in order to create a sense of unity and a shared desire for transformation and commitment to reverse the culture of divisiveness.

The training consisted of discussions, reflective analyses, and small lectures, with the goal of raising youths' consciousness by identifying and exploring their beliefs and misunderstandings that had led to misconceptions and distrust. The intercommunity dialogues included an examination of the realities of self-destructive violent rivalries. More important, these discussions focused on the core rationale and meaning behind youth violence. These reflective exercises bridged the gap between rival youths' needs and values, creating a new identity that would reinforce unity and lead to a commitment to nonviolence. Paulo Freire emphatically portrays this realization as creating a "horizontal relation" that uses sustained dialogue to create mutual trust and partnership for action.[8]

Training seminars. To transform violent interaction into nonviolent methods of action requires introducing a new mind-set and new ways to interact. The trainers provided practical applications for nonviolent methods of action. The peace-building training seminars equipped participants with skills in negotiation, mediation, nonviolent methods, community organization, and leadership. Developing these new skills would give youth a sense of security, control, and fulfillment in this transitional period.

These skills are vital components of YIPP's success. Members need to apply these skills in their daily lives as they confront the challenge of persuading young people to abandon violence and instead engage in nonviolent methods of action. YIPP members identified five principles for nonviolence by which they would abide:

1. Actively love the country and its people.
2. Act respectfully at all times.
3. Have the courage to examine oneself.
4. Be ready to compromise.
5. Act in the face of an unjust act.

Evaluation and reaction. Workshop sessions ended with an evaluation of the training materials by the participants. The initial workshop, as well as subsequent intercommunity dialogues and training seminars, have been met with interest and enthusiasm. The responses after the training have shown a sense of unity and shared aspiration to end the cycle of violence. As one participant explained, "Now that we have become one family, we should care for one another on the street, at work, in our community." Another participant echoed this response, noting that YIPP came at the right moment when many young people feel hopeless, disoriented and manipulated.

Some participants expressed concerns about the reaction of political authorities, who might use force to undermine the goals of YIPP. Because of their prolonged experience with coercive force and a culture of intimidation, participants saw this potential challenge as a real concern.

Organizational structure. YIPP's founder and principal organizer and trainer is a native of Burundi and survivor of the conflicts in both Burundi and Rwanda. His personal experience in both conflicts has led him to understand the role that youth play in the perpetuation of interethnic violence. He focused his graduate studies in international peace building at the University of Notre Dame, gaining the intellectual framework for designing YIPP, as well as for developing its training materials.

The organization has the following structure:

- Executive committee. This group consists of the ten founding members, who come from different ethnic backgrounds and various local communities of Bujumbura. Their responsibilities in YIPP vary with respect to their experience and skills.
- Operational corps. The six individuals in the operational corps are responsible for conducting workshops in nonviolence training, collecting resources, and providing the logistics. They also serve as trainers for focal point leaders and coordinators of cross-community and district nonviolence activities. In addition, they develop media strategies to promote the project and spread the call for nonviolent action.
- Focal point leadership. With the goal of reversing the downward spiral of communal violence, YIPP has established focal point leadership for each district of Bujumbura. The leaders, who have participated in YIPP workshops, have the following tasks:

- Mobilizing and recruiting young people in their communities to participate in community peace dialogue sessions and peace-building training seminars
- Recruiting young people to adhere to the movement of nonviolence
- Creating an organizational structure at each focal point level to strengthen YIPP focal points

- Assessing the needs and concerns of their respective communities for possible intervention
- With direction from the operational corps, creating intercommunity projects that aim to reinforce the message of YIPP
- Mobilizing members for intercommunity events to encourage interaction, cooperation, and collaboration between all ethnic groups in all focal points

Effective training of focal point leadership has been key to YIPP's impact on the community. Through its focal points, YIPP has begun to establish a network of intercommunity peace dialogues. A visible impact of the effectiveness of these intercommunity peace dialogues and training seminars at the focal point level is the increased number of young people adhering to the project's principles. Another result has been the request by many university students to expand YIPP in the countryside by creating YIPP focal points in their native provinces.

YIPP's focal points have been able to penetrate communities, resulting in unprecedented intercommunity social activities. For example, members of YIPP from a predominantly Tutsi zone, where Hutu residents and visitors have previously been burned to death, invited focal point representatives from predominantly Hutu zones for a social event. At the event, members from both zones socialized and sang a song of peace. This symbolic event has had a significant impression on both communities.

Youth peace clubs

Following the establishment of focal point leadership, YIPP started to organize youth peace clubs in each district of Bujumbura. These clubs provide activities for youth and promote dialogue on issues relevant to their well-being. The clubs give the young people a sense of belonging to the community, provide them with the opportunity to develop their talents together, and display the importance of team effort as well as mutual dependency.

YIPP has already established traditional arts clubs for dancers and musicians, and it is working to organize a variety of other clubs, including tutoring clubs, athletic clubs, traditional arts clubs, employment and volunteer clubs, as well as democracy and human rights clubs. The first demonstration of their success was at YIPP's New Year's Celebration of Peace, which took place in Bujumbura on December 31, 2003. The Celebration of Peace united an estimated two thousand young Burundians from both ethnic groups, representing all zones of Bujumbura, for a soccer game featuring mixed Hutu-Tutsi teams and performances by traditional dance and drum teams from both ethnicities. The celebration reinforced the spirit of collaboration and the sense of togetherness in voicing young people's aspirations for reconciliation and peaceful coexistence.

Community service

In an effort to address community needs, YIPP's focal point leaders, with the help of the operational corps, coordinate young people who are assisting in rebuilding communities, especially during their summer vacations. Youth from all ethnic groups have made plans to rebuild houses, particularly those of families who are known to be victims of selective acts of ethnic violence. Selected groups of young people from focal points of predominantly Tutsi zones will join their peers of predominantly Hutu zones to clear land and rebuild communities. Other focal point leaders have been working in rural areas to help farmers with their fieldwork.

Since most communities have become segregated as a result of the prolonged communal violence, these intercommunity activities and networking are essential to the diffusion of tension, the rebuilding of relationships, and the achievement of social reconciliation. In this way, the process of physical and emotional healing for the community, as well as for individuals, is beginning. As young people work toward community and nation building, they feel valued and experience a renewed sense of meaning and fulfillment.

Rehabilitation and integration

YIPP has designed each focal point to be a welcoming body that will support, rehabilitate, and integrate young people returning from refugee and displacement camps as well as those who have been combatants. This is a communal interventional process where members of YIPP provide support for returnees.

For refugees returning home, YIPP's focal points mobilize members in their respective communities to provide emotional and material support. Children and youth are integrated in youth peace clubs to provide them with educational preparation to enroll in formal school or professional skills development training and guidance for economic self-sufficiency. YIPP has a growing number of university students ready to provide tutoring, and it is developing a group of professional volunteers to instruct youth in technical skills development. These YIPP welcoming bodies in each community for the returnees also serve to diffuse suspicions and address any negativity associated with refugees, displaced people, ex-combatants, and former militia returning to their communities.

YIPP is working with local academic institutions, psychology departments, and other resources to establish a network of students and academic professionals to provide healing and counseling services for these youth. Since YIPP seeks to be a sustainable nonviolence social movement that addresses community needs and concerns, its networking with academic institutions will help mobilize the intellectual communities in providing resources to address community challenges.

Challenges confronting the Youth Intervention for Peace Project

The practical application of conflict resolution skills and programs in Burundi has helped to restore relationships and contain youth violence. At the same time, it has identified some challenges.

YIPP faces two major obstacles. First, it has had to address potential struggles of power within the organization. As often happens in interventions, the more educated participants tend to monopolize the process and disregard the less educated. This struggle could disrupt the core principles of YIPP. YIPP has developed a code of conduct for its members, and all are expected to use effective and transparent communication to express concerns and address problems.

Second, adequate funding remains a key dilemma. Because most funding is directed to top-level interventions or initiatives organized by outside groups, YIPP has struggled to attract funding to support its program. Currently, it depends completely on local and outside individual contributions to support its programs. Volunteerism is the backbone of its operations.

Although funding difficulties have slowed YIPP's progress, it has also had an unanticipated positive effect. Locally, YIPP is perceived as a project of necessity that will have a long-term sustainable impact, rather than a "profit ride" project whose members' primary motivation is to profit individually. The plans that many other international organizations have developed that provide monetary incentives or rewards to participants in peace-building activities aimed at benefiting society have actually had a negative impact on Burundian society; they have promoted a culture that expects individual financial gain as a result of participating in these projects.

Facing the future

To provide effective conflict management in intergroup conflict, the fundamental needs, values, interests, and concerns of youth engaging in ethnic violence must be addressed. Programs aimed at reversing this violence need to provide youth with an active role in the resolution of the conflict and a defined responsibility in community and nation building. Activities should not focus simply on recreation or life skills development, but rather should empower young people with a vision for transformation and new avenues to participate in their community and nation socially, politically, and economically.

The long-term goal for YIPP is to strengthen and improve youth participation in the civic and political areas of life Burundi. By encouraging youth to escape the cycle of violence and empowering them with the skills they need to be contributing community members and citizens, YIPP is helping Burundi move toward a peaceful and promising future.

Notes

1. See http://news.bbc.co.uk/2/hi/africa/country_profiles/1068873.stm.

2. See Burundi: Analysts warn of serious political deterioration. (2003, Feb. 15–21). Integrated Regional Information Network for Central and Eastern Africa, Weekly Round-Up 162.

3. Allis, J. (2003, May 1). Fear and fury cast over Burundi peace. *Guardian International.* Available on-line: http://www.guardian.co.uk/international/story/0,3604,946861,00.html.

4. Lemarchand, R. (1996). *Burundi: Ethnic Conflict and Genocide.* New York: Woodrow Wilson Center Press and Cambridge University Press. P. 6.

5. United Nations Secretary-General. (2000, July.). Children and armed conflict. In *United Nations Report 2000.* New York: United Nations.

6. Kelman, H. C. (1997) Social-psychological dimensions of international conflict. In W. I. Zartman & L. J. Rasmussen (Eds.), *Peacemaking in international conflict: Method and techniques.* Washington, DC: U.S. Institute for Peace Press. P. 197.

7. Lederach, J. P. (1996). *Preparing for peace: Conflict transformation across cultures.* Syracuse, NY: Syracuse University Press.

8. Freire, P. (2001). *Pedagogy of the oppressed* (M. B. Ramos, Trans., 30th anniversary ed.). New York: Continuum International.

JEAN-PAUL BIGIRINDAVYI *is the founder and director of the Youth Intervention for Peace Project and a native Burundian.*

Social identity is multilayered and complex. Schools, communities, and nations can implement structures and approaches that help youth to understand one another and respect differences.

6

Challenging intolerance

Alan Smith, Ciarán Ó Maoláin

SINCE INTOLERANCE RELATES primarily to intergroup relations, it is important to begin from an awareness of how group identity is constructed and reproduced. Here, it may be useful to compare the identity, or rather the overlapping set of identities, of each individual with a technique used by map makers. When we look at a modern map, we are confronted with several layers of meaning: we see natural boundaries such as shores and rivers, political boundaries such as international borders and administrative regions, coloring to represent vegetation or physical contours, the naming of places, and the networks of communication that connect them. In the mapmaking process, these various layers of information, the different ways of seeing the same geographical region, may be drawn up separately on a set of plates called palimpsests. Only by printing all the palimpsests on one sheet of paper can we get a full view of the complexity of the environment in which we live. The same word, incidentally, is used to describe manuscripts in which parts have been written, erased, and written over again. In that sense it is useful in conceptualizing the way in which cultures and identities, often perceived as immutable, modulate and redefine themselves over time. Culture is an acquired collection of beliefs, practices, and social

NEW DIRECTIONS FOR YOUTH DEVELOPMENT, NO. 102, SUMMER 2004 © WILEY PERIODICALS, INC.

institutions inherited from previous generations. We are trained to accept our culture as a given, as a natural part of our environment, and to use it as a yardstick against which we evaluate the cultures of others. The great danger is that we do not choose to, or are not trained to, question our cultural inheritance, that we do not recognize or readily accept the evolutions and mutations that occur in our culture, and that our given notion of what constitutes our culture is deemed to be beyond rational criticism.

In much the same way, the social identity of the individual is a complex layering and may include different classes of physical characteristics; local, regional, and national belongings; affiliations to particular religions, cultures, and political and philosophical ideas; socioeconomic status; level of education; style of life, and so on. Thus, a person is defined partly in terms of the characteristics with which he or she was born: male or female; black or white; ablebodied or with congenital or acquired disabilities. However, one can acquire through a process of acculturation, or in later life through a series of intellectual choices, a much wider range of identities. In Northern Ireland, it is common to be acculturated as an Irish Catholic or British Protestant or a combination of these; these are identities that are not particularly easy to shake off. Most of us have a loyalty to family, neighborhood, and the city where we live. We may identify with our country, although for those born in Northern Ireland, the term *country* can have different interpretations. Each of us may have a political orientation, a sexual orientation, an attachment to family, an identity connected with an age group, employment, and social class. These various identities do not contradict one another; they coexist, overlap, and interact with one another.

Many such layers of identity derive from the accident of birth or from other factors outside the control of the individual and, to some extent, factors such as religion, employment status, and family status. Still other forms of identity are those imposed on us by others. Those from outside a particular identity group do not always choose to perceive or identify members of the group by the same criteria and terminology as the members use for themselves. Such misnamings are invariably negative, ranging from simple cultural misunderstanding, through a refusal to accept the validity of the criteria used by the group, to, at the most extreme level, a decision to substitute the chosen identity with a negative, stereotypical, or derogatory usage. The systematic suppression of national cultural expression in eastern Europe is a recent example of the contesting of the validity of group identities; similarly, "Nigger," "Yid," "Paddy," "tinker," and "cripple" are all examples of imposed identities derived from insensitivity and intolerance. It might also be argued that in Northern Ireland, at least until very recently, there was a refusal at the official level to recognize the legitimacy of the identity of a very large sector of the population.

We stress the complexity of social identity because manifestations of intolerance occur around every facet of that social identity: religion or belief, race or skin color, political allegiance, nationality, citizenship and immigration status, age, social class, gender, sexuality, ability or disability, lifestyle. We have developed a vocabulary to describe each form of intolerance and its social expressions: racism, sexism, sectarianism, anti-Semitism, xenophobia, chauvinism, and, in recent years, the more contested concepts of ageism, ableism, cultural imperialism, heterosexism, and others. Some of these expressions of intolerance occur in an isolated, informal, incidental way, as in acts of discrimination against individuals by individuals; other forms elevate group identity into an ideology, as in the formation of racist political parties. In between the extremes of casual discrimination and ideological supremacism are countless gradations, including the adoption by mainstream political parties and governments of policies that are discriminatory in intent or application. The term *intolerance* may be applied across this whole range of experiences: it means, in essence, the sacralization of the boundaries between social groups, giving rise to doctrines of superiority and discourses of irrational fear and prejudice. This sanctions discrimination in employment and other social relations, oppression by the state, and aggressive behavior by state or private entities toward members of minorities or out-groups.

With so many forms of group identification and differentiation, conflict between groups is inevitable. Conflict is not always destructive; the challenging of one cultural form by another, and their creative interaction, can be one of the most productive and positive dynamics of social life. Instead, our primary concern is the social control of conflict and, in particular, prevention of the exercise of cultural, political, and ethnic hegemony by any one group or by a majority in a society to the extent that it infringes on the right of any less powerful group to own, express, and assert its own identity. It is incumbent on every state to provide controls and guarantees to protect the rights of minorities, provide redress against infringement of those rights, and create the conditions and the mechanisms that reinforce intergroup tolerance and understanding.

Education and youth work initiatives

There are numerous institutional and social controls on intolerance, including legal controls, regulatory and administrative controls, community relations work by the state, and cultural action against intolerance. Beyond these, education and youth work programs form an essential element of efforts to combat intolerance.

There can be no standard international formula for the development of education and youth work initiatives to combat intolerance. Each country, and each education and youth work system within that country, must work to provide programs that reflect the specificity of their national circumstances. In Spain, there have been largely successful attempts to develop educational systems that respect the linguistic and cultural autonomy of regions such as Euskadi and Catalunya, but debates at the national level about the political autonomy of the regions versus the concept of the Spanish State still affect young people and give rise to conflict among them. There are also important questions concerning the rights of North African migrant workers.

In Portugal, as in Spain, there is a relatively recent memory of authoritarian oppressive government, and despite its relatively homogeneous population, in terms of language, ethnicity, and religion, there is a sense that it has not come fully to terms with its colonial past and the ongoing obligations that creates. In Lithuania, the problems are different; there are ethnolinguistic minorities of Russian, Polish, and Belorussian origin. In Romania, the problems of intergroup relations may concern external minorities, such as the Romanian-speaking population in Moldova, or national minorities such as the Hungarian- and German-speaking groups.

In the Czech Republic and Slovakia, the main issue is in giving expression to the decision to separate a binational state, while respecting the rights of Slovak and Czech minorities within each nation, those of the considerable number of binational families and those of the Hungarian and Romany minorities in Slovakia. In many east European states, there are conflicts, often of an intergenerational nature, between those who have adapted, to greater or lesser degrees, to the transition from communism. We should not underestimate the traumatic extent to which changes create a resistance to cultural evolution and fuel racism and xenophobia alongside the more healthy expressions of confident nationalism. It is an unfortunate fact that resurgent nationalisms provide a political space where those who espouse noninclusive, fundamentalist concepts of purely ethnic nationhood can flourish.

Despite the many differences to be observed among European jurisdictions, what they have in common is the existence of a long tradition of racism, a degree of anti-Semitism, a limited toleration of national minorities and migrant communities, and a certain sense of cultural superiority over non-European peoples.

Programs to promote respect for diversity

Turning now to specific programs that have been applied, these can be grouped in three broad areas. The first is institutional change, that is, the creation of new systems of schooling that attempt to cater to the needs of a pluralist society. The second is curriculum change, that is, the modification or wholesale reform of the school curriculum to introduce themes or methodologies designed to ameliorate intergroup relations. The third is single-community and cross-community youth work, that is, the bringing together of young people outside the educational system, either within their own ethnic communities or in ethnically mixed groups, to promote mutual understanding at individual and intercommunal levels.

Institutional change

The first group of initiatives has two forms that at first sight are contradictory in their nature. One involves creating separate schooling systems to cater for separate ethnic communities. The other is based on integrated philosophies, that is, the bringing together of different ethnic communities within a common school system and with a shared curriculum.

In Northern Ireland, the vast majority of Protestant children attend state-controlled schools, which are staffed almost exclusively by Protestants; most Catholic children attend schools in the voluntary maintained sector, which are staffed almost exclusively by Catholics. In the past, this division was justified by its proponents on the basis that each of the two communities had its own historical tradition and religious ethos and had the fundamental right to transmit that culture to the next generation. For example, the history taught in Catholic schools was basically Irish history, and Catholic social teaching influenced the content of the curriculum in many areas. Irish language was taught, traditional Irish sports were played, and religious rites of passage, such as First Communion and Confirmation, were very much a part of the everyday life of the schools. In the Protestant schools, the core of the history syllabus was British history, the British flag and portraits of the queen were displayed, British sports were played, and although the syllabus was officially secular, a distinctly Protestant ethos prevailed. Undoubtedly, the separation of the systems succeeded in maintaining the separate identity of the two communities, but at the same time, it greatly reduced the opportunities for children from the two communities to mix together and come to understand one another. The separate institutional structures also perpetuated inequities between the two communities; for example, the Protestant state schools received higher funding than the Catholic schools, and this resulted in Catholics' having fewer educational qualifications and hence fewer employment opportunities.

A second example comes from Great Britain, where most education is through a secular state system. One minority group there that has mounted a vigorous campaign for state funding of its own school system is the Muslim population, consisting largely of immigrants from the Indian subcontinent and their families. Many Muslims have felt that the secular ethos of state schools and the education together of boys and girls are contrary to Muslim precepts and endanger the survival of their religion and the Islamic way of life. Some voluntary Islamic schools have been created, and the demand now is that these schools should be entitled to full state funding, on the same basis as the Catholic and Jewish schools. The issue is presented as one of civil rights: specifically, the right of a minority to reproduce its culture through education.

The third, and perhaps most successful, example of institutional reform comes from Spain, or rather the Basque country. It has developed a novel approach to accommodate the linguistic differences in its population. There is still a single state-funded school system, but within that system, and indeed within each school, parents select from three different streaming systems for their children. One has every subject taught through Spanish; another has every subject taught through the Basque language, Euskerra; and a third system has the two languages used for different subjects. In each case, the curriculum is identical; only the medium of instruction is open to choice.

The debate is the extent to which the state has an obligation to provide equal levels of funding and support to education tailored to the cultural, ethnic, religious, or linguistic backgrounds of minorities and the extent to which such provision constitutes a recognition of basic human rights or a mechanism for perpetuating division and intolerance. There are no easy answers, but in situations where the state system is clearly shown to be incapable of or unwilling to respond to the needs of minority students, then minorities will seek to develop their own school systems. The other major option is the creation, where these do not already exist, of schools that deliberately set out to bring together children from different ethnic or community backgrounds, that is, to raise together children who would ordinarily be separated and to give them a shared educational background in the hope that in later life, they will be readier to associate with one another and will find it easier to resolve their differences. One example of deliberately transformative education is seen in the integrated schools movement in Northern Ireland. The first planned, integrated school in Northern Ireland opened in 1981. It was planned in the sense that the school structures are designed to secure equal representation from the Catholic and Protestant communities within the management, staffing and enrollment of the school. By 2003, there were fifty integrated schools (thirty-two primary and eighteen colleges) attended by 16,575 pupils (5 percent of the school population). Initially, the government did not fund these schools, but legislation now requires the government to support integrated education by funding new integrated schools and by allowing existing schools to become integrated. The emphasis in Northern Ireland has been on voluntary integration with parental consent rather than a government policy that introduces compulsory desegregation.[1]

Curricular reform

As well as institutional change, another approach is the reform of the school curriculum in ways designed to improve intergroup relations. Of course, this must involve both a reform of teacher training systems and the development of in-service training for teachers already working, so any initiative in this field will be expensive and will take many years to institutionalize. A number of examples from Northern Ireland have developed as responses to the communal violence of the past thirty years. The first is the development of formal and informal links between schools, which may be in curriculum areas or in cultural or sports activities. After a series of research projects and pilot programs, the government decided to fund from 1987 a scheme that promoted interschool contact. At present, about a third of Catholic and Protestant primary schools and about half of the postprimary schools participate in the plan in areas such as joint fieldwork on local history and areas of cultural difference.

Another initiative was the introduction as a cross-curricular theme (one that is supposed to influence the teaching of every subject) of education for mutual understanding (EMU). This concept, developed in the early 1980s, was imposed as a statutory requirement on all schools as part of a general curriculum reform from 1989. The aims of EMU have been to enable young people to learn respect for themselves and others, appreciate the interdependence of people within society, know about and understand what is shared as well as what is different about their cultural traditions, and appreciate how conflict may be handled in nonviolent ways. An evaluation of EMU suggested some weaknesses in this approach and that many schools were adopting a minimalist approach.[2] In particular, it was suggested that EMU was not addressing important social, cultural, and political issues that have a bearing on community relations in Northern Ireland. Teachers still expressed considerable reservations about addressing issues such as violence and sectarianism.

However, there has been further progression in thinking about curriculum change, particularly since the peace process that led to the Belfast (Good Friday) Agreement in April 1998. The establishment of new political institutions created a rationale for an education program that introduces young people to concepts of democracy and encourages their participation in civil society. New equality legislation further underlined the need for education programs that introduce young people to human rights principles. A pilot program for citizenship education has been underway since 1998, and this has now been adopted as part of the future curriculum for all schools. The program is based on the investigation of core concepts related to diversity and inclusion, equality and justice, rights and responsibilities, and democracy and participation. It is extremely important that the program is an inquiry-based model of curriculum.[3] This means that the core concepts are regarded as problematic from the outset and explored from multiple perspectives through a range of local and international issues. Although there is a knowledge component, there is not an emphasis on prescribing civic facts that have to be taught. The political context also has significant implications for the model of citizenship education that is emerging in Northern Ireland. A "patriotic" model of citizenship that simply promotes loyalty to the state would be inappropriate in a situation where the concept of nationality is a divisive issue, so alternative models of multiple citizenship need to be explored.

Youth work

Before discussing specific types of youth work, it is important to stress two things. The first is the importance of work outside the school context, especially in communities and age groups where the influence of the school is limited, for example, among sixteen to eighteen year olds who have left school. The second point is the importance of the adoption by national and local youth agencies of an overt and detailed policy of opposing discrimination and intolerance and promoting good intergroup relations. There are already many instances of this, for example, the inclusion of a community relations remit in the functions of the Youth Council for Northern Ireland when it was formed in 1990. This reflected an earlier, 1987, policy for the youth service in the region, and it is now accepted that a central aim of state-funded youth work should be to promote understanding of diversity and communication across social boundaries.

In societies with what are broadly termed ethnic divisions, whether these are along racial, linguistic, religious, or other lines, it is often the case that youth organizations serve particular ethnic communities. That is especially so in the case of locally based organizations when there is a high level of ethnic residential segregation, as is the case in Northern Ireland. Consequently, one of the major forms of cross-community youth work involves the bringing together of two or more groups from different communities for joint activities. In Northern Ireland, funding and other support for such intercommunity activities may be obtained from a variety of sources, including since 1987 the Department of Education, the Community Relations Council, charitable funders, and local government. As with interschools work, it is preferable to emphasize cooperative methodologies rather than those of a competitive nature, such as team sports pitting one community against the other.

Recent research in Northern Ireland has pointed to major difficulties in using youth sports as a vehicle for improving community relations. The first problem is that many sports are more or less exclusively played in one or other of the communities, and among those sports with followings in both communities, particular teams tend to draw their support from their community or the other. This is partly a consequence of residential segregation and the identification of teams with the segregated locality in which they have their grounds. There are a number of initiatives designed to create integrated teams in sports, such as rugby and basketball, but even if these are successful, they can attract opposition on the grounds that they undermine the established, segregated sporting traditions. Nonteam sports, such as boxing, are relatively immune from sectarian division, but their individualistic nature makes them unsuitable for bringing people together with anything other than a strictly sporting agenda.

In addition to the local groups in Northern Ireland, there are a large number of regionwide organizations that either work exclusively in the field of youth community relations or include work with children and young people as part of a general community relations remit. Many of these play the role of facilitator, bringing the local groups together, while others work independently. Problems in intercommunity youth work in Northern Ireland, for both the regional bodies and local groups, have included the shortage of neutral venues: most of the possible meeting facilities are owned by or identified with one community or the other. Another difficulty, particularly in relation to work funded through local government, has been the difficulty of persuading many of those involved to see the core problem in Northern Ireland as one of community divisions. In the more peaceful areas, the conflict tends to be seen in terms of fighting among extremist factions in other areas, and the relevance of bringing young people together can be questioned. Youth work is seen as competing for resources with other, perhaps more urgent, areas of social need, and there can be resentment if it is seen as diverting funding. There is also a lack of cohesion in the way that community relations funding has been applied, with a great deal of spending on one-off, spectacular events with little or no long-term benefit: cross-community carnivals, arts events, and so on. Similarly, some community relations funding has been applied to substitute for other budget headings, for example to pay for Christmas lights.

Despite all these problems, much useful work gets done. Examples of successful community relations spending include the development of cross-community economic development groups, often with an emphasis on combating youth unemployment; the funding of cultural groups in amateur drama, local history, music, and so on; and a relatively small amount of more focused prejudice reduction and antisectarianism group work. Although not all of these initiatives have been directed solely at young people, they tend to have a high degree of involvement in many of them.

At least in Northern Ireland, practitioners and researchers in the youth work field agree on some of the main criteria for progress in any youth work around issues of division and tolerance. For example, the young people must be provided with a safe environment in which to discuss the issues, and the format of discussion must minimize the stressfulness of the experience; they must be given the opportunity to talk as well as to listen; there should be an emphasis on positive themes rather than conflictual ones; and the discussions should be aimed at encouraging young people to make decisions and to reflect on how personal choices can influence the wider society. A model that has been developed by the Northern Ireland youth agencies suggests that it is important not to try to address all the issues at once, but to start with a general exploration of social diversity and move on gradually to more controversial issues, culminating in an exploration of the psychology of conflict and, finally, introducing conflict resolution theory and possible solutions.[4] Alongside such an approach is the need to develop greater confidence and competence among teachers and youth workers in facilitating the discussion of potentially controversial issues. This means taking account of the emotional dimensions of intercultural learn-ing, developing an awareness of the various roles that the facilita-tor can adopt, and recognizing the need to draw on personal biography as a learning resource. Many of these issues have been explored through development projects with young people in Northern Ireland.[5]

The fundamental problem with any attempt to address issues of intolerance, inequality, and discrimination through working with young people is that youth work takes place in societies that are not controlled by young people. Even if we succeed in providing a very large number of young people with the information and concep-tual tools, we have to recognize that outside the education and youth work contexts they are immersed in, and susceptible to, a vast range of cultural influences undermine tolerance. This means that as well as working on the attitudes of young people, we must always work at many other levels to reduce intergroup tensions in society and to promote interaction and mutual understanding. We must change discriminatory institutional structures and challenge inequitable public policies and individual acts of intolerance. The aim of any project or initiative should not be overly ambitious; even the most sophisticated, long-term, fully funded work with young people is unlikely to bring about a complete reversal of intolerant attitudes. We should be content if we succeed first in increasing young people's experience of positive forms of intergroup contact and then in inspiring them to adopt a more critical approach to received wisdoms. The point is not to change young people but to enable them to change.

Notes

1. Smith, A. (2001). Religious segregation and the emergence of integrated schools in Northern Ireland. *Oxford Review of Education, 27,* 559–575.

2. Smith, A., & Robinson, A. (1996). *Education for mutual understanding: The statutory years.* Coleraine: Centre for the Study of Conflict, University of Ulster. Available at: www.cain.ulster.ac.uk.

3. Smith, A. (2003). Citizenship education in Northern Ireland: Beyond national identity? *Cambridge Journal of Education, 33,* 15–31.

4. Youth Council for Northern Ireland. (1992). *Community relations guide-lines: Youth work curriculum.* Belfast: Author.

5. McCully, A., O'Doherty, M., & Smyth, P. (1999). Exploring controversial issues in Northern Ireland. In L. Forcey & I. Harris (Eds.), *Peacebuilding for adolescents: Strategies for teachers and community leaders* (pp. 119–138). New York: Peter Lang.

ALAN SMITH *holds a UNESCO chair in Education for Pluralism, Human Rights and Democracy at the University of Ulster, Northern Ireland.*

CIARÁN Ó MAOLÁIN *is a research worker with the Northern Ireland Human Rights Commission.*

Index

Notes for Contributors

New Directions for Youth Development: Theory, Practice, and Research is a quarterly publication focusing on current contemporary issues challenging the field of youth development. A defining focus of the journal is the relationship among theory, research, and practice. In particular, *NDYD* is dedicated to recognizing resilience as well as risk, and healthy development of our youth as well as the difficulties of adolescence. The journal is intended as a forum for provocative discussion that reaches across the worlds of academia, service, philanthropy, and policy.

In the tradition of the New Directions series, each volume of the journal addresses a single, timely topic, although special issues covering a variety of topics are occasionally commissioned. We welcome submissions of both volume topics and individual articles. All articles should specifically address the implications of theory for practice and research directions, and how these arenas can better inform one another. Articles may focus on any aspect of youth development; all theoretical and methodological orientations are welcome.

If you would like to be an *issue editor*, please submit an outline of no more than four pages (single spaced, 12 point type) that includes a brief description of your proposed topic and its significance along with a brief synopsis of individual articles (including tentative authors and a working title for each chapter).

If you would like to be an *author*, please submit first a draft of an abstract of no more than 1,500 words, including a two-sentence synopsis of the article; send this to the managing editor.

For all prospective issue editors or authors:

- Please make sure to keep accessibility in mind, by illustrating theoretical ideas with specific examples and explaining technical terms in nontechnical language. A busy practitioner who may not have an extensive research background should be well served by our work.

- Please keep in mind that references should be limited to twenty-five to thirty. Authors should make use of case examples to illustrate their ideas, rather than citing exhaustive research references. You may want to recommend two or three key articles, books, or Websites that are influential in the field, to be featured on a resource page. This can be used by readers who want to delve more deeply into a particular topic.

- All reference information should be listed as endnotes, rather than including author names in the body of the article or footnotes at the bottom of the page.

Back Issue/Subscription Order Form

Copy or detach and send to:

Jossey-Bass, A Wiley Imprint, 989 Market Street, San Francisco CA 94103-1741

Call or fax toll-free: Phone 888-378-2537; Fax 888-481-2665

Back Issues: Please send me the following issues at $29 each
(Important: please include issue ISBN)

_____

_____

$ _____   Total for single issues

$ _____   SHIPPING CHARGES: SURFACE   Domestic Canadian
First Item $5.00 $6.00
Each Add'l Item $3.00 $1.50
Please call for next day, second day, or international shipping rates.

Subscriptions   Please ❏ start ❏ renew my subscription to _New Directions for Youth Development_ at the following rate:

U.S.	❏ Individual $80	❏ Institutional $160
Canada	❏ Individual $80	❏ Institutional $200
All Others	❏ Individual $104	❏ Institutional $234
Online Subscription		❏ Institutional $176

**For more information about online subscriptions visit
www.interscience.wiley.com**

-- _____   Are you eligible for our **Student Subscription Rate**? Attach a copy of your current Student Identification Card and deduct 20% from the regular subscription rate.

$ _____   Total single issues and subscriptions (Add appropriate sales tax for your state for single issue orders. No sales tax for U.S. subscriptions. Canadian residents, add GST for subscriptions and single issues.)

❏Payment enclosed (U.S. check or money order only)
❏VISA ❏ MC ❏ AmEx # _____ Exp. Date _____
Your credit card payment will be charged to John Wiley & Sons.

Signature _____ Day Phone _____
❏ Bill Me (U.S. institutional orders only. Purchase order required.)

Purchase order # _____
Federal Tax ID13559302   **GST 89102 8052**

Name _____

Address _____

_____

Phone _____ E-mail _____

Other Titles Available

NEW DIRECTIONS FOR YOUTH DEVELOPMENT: THEORY, PRACTICE, AND RESEARCH
Gil G. Noam, Editor-in-Chief

YD101 **After-School Worlds: Creating a New Social Space for Development and Learning**
Gil G. Noam
Showcases a variety of large-scale policy initiatives, effective institutional collaborations, and innovative programming options that produce high-quality environments in which young people are realizing their potential. Contributors underscore the conditions—from fostering interagency partnerships, to structuring organized out-of-school-time activities, to encouraging staff-student relationships—that lay the groundwork for positive youth development after school. At the same time, their examples illuminate the challenges for policymakers, researchers, and educators to redefine the field of afterschool as a whole, including the search for a shared lexicon, the push to preserve the character of after-school as an intermediary space, and the need to create and further programs that are grounded in reliable research and that demonstrate success.
ISBN 0-7879-7304-1

YD100 **Understanding the Social Worlds of Immigrant Youth**
Carola Suárez-Orozco, Irina L. G. Todorova
This issue seeks to deepen understanding of the major social influences that shape immigrant youths' paths in their transition to the United States. The authors delve into a number of social worlds that can contribute to the positive development of immigrant youth. They also provide insight into sources of information about identity pathway options available to those youth. The chapters offer new data regarding the developmental opportunities that family roles and responsibilities, school contexts, community organizations, religious involvement and beliefs, gendered expectations, and media influences present.
ISBN 0-7879-7267-3

YD99 **Deconstructing the School-to-Prison Pipeline**
Johanna Wald, Daniel J. Losen
This issue describes how school policies can have the effect, if not the intent, of setting youths on the "prison track." It also identifies programs and policies that can help schools maintain safety and order while simultaneously reaching out to those students most in need of structure, education, and guidance. Offering a balanced per-

spective, this issue begins to point the way toward less punitive, more effective, hopeful directions.
ISBN 0-7879-7227-4

YD98   **Youth Facing Threat and Terror: Supporting Preparedness and Resilience**
Robert D. Macy, Susanna Barry, Gil G. Noam
Intended to help clinicians, youth and community workers, teachers, and parents to support resolution and recovery, this volume examines the effects of threat, stress, and traumatic events, including acts of terror, on children and youth. It addresses not only the individual repercussions of threat but also a collective approach to threat. It also illustrates important ways to prevent traumatic situations from having lifelong, negative impacts. These methods involve providing immediate intervention and fostering safety as soon as a threatening incident has occurred as well as preparing children for future threats in ways that enhance feelings of safety rather than raise anxiety.
ISBN 0-7879-7075-1

YD97   **When, Where, What, and How Youth Learn**
Karen J. Pittman, Nicole Yohalem, Joel Tolman
Acknowledging that young people learn throughout their waking hours, in a range of settings, and through a variety of means, this volume presents practical advancements, theory development and new research in policies and infrastructures that support expanded definitions of learning. Representing the perspectives of a broad range of scholars and practitioners, chapters explore ways to connect learning experiences that happen inside and outside school buildings and during and after the school day. The contributors offer a compelling argument that communitywide commitments to learning are necessary if our nation's young people are to become problem free, fully prepared, and fully engaged.
ISBN 0-7879-6848-X

YD96   **Youth Participation: Improving Institutions and Communities**
Benjamin Kirshner, Jennifer L. O'Donoghue, Milbrey McLaughlin
Explores the growing effort in youth organizations, community development, and schools and other public institutions to foster meaningful activities that empower adolescents to participate in decision making that affects their lives and to take action on issues they care about. Pushing against long-held, culturally specific ideas about adolescence as well as institutional barriers to youth involvement, the efforts of these organizations engaged in youth participation programs deserve careful analysis and support. This volume offers an assessment of the field, as well as specific chapters that chronicle efforts to achieve youth participation across a variety of settings and dimensions.
ISBN 0-7879-6339-9